W9-DAU-943

Landslide

Landslide

The how & why of Nixon's victory

By ARTHUR PEARL

THE CITADEL PRESS   SECAUCUS, NEW JERSEY

First edition
Copyright © 1973 by Arthur Pearl
All rights reserved
Published by Citadel Press
A division of Lyle Stuart, Inc.
120 Enterprise Ave., Secaucus, N. J. 07094
In Canada: George J. McLeod Limited
73 Bathurst St., Toronto 2B, Ontario
Manufactured in the United States of America
Library of Congress catalog card number: 73-84147
ISBN 0-8065-0382-3

Dedicated to WAYNE MORSE,
a man with a terrible language handicap.
He never learned the meaning
of the word "quit."

Contents

1 Landslide—or Mudslide   *11*

2 Voting as a psychological phenomenon—or, How an oleaginous blob becomes perfectly clear   *23*

3 Fooling as a function of foolishness—or, A rolling stone is a political force   *39*

4 A new majority in every mirage—or, Kissinger as Merlin, Sammy Davis, Jr., as the White Knight   *55*

5 War is peace—or, How the Grinch stole Christmas   *73*

6 Any able-bodied man can—or, With all that unemployment there must be jobs somewhere   *105*

7 The quality of life *is* strained—or, There is more to life than war or work   *163*

8 Th-th-they th-th-threw me off th-th-the d-d-debate t-t-team be-b-because I was J-J-J-Jewish—or, Maybe Nixon didn't win, maybe McGovern lost   *191*

9 The boys in the bandwagon—or, A slick poll-ish joke   *207*

10 Watergate—the blot that wouldn't go away—or, The last tangle on the Potomac   *215*

11 A jump toward a conclusion—or, Will 1984 be here before 1976?   *235*

Landslide

CHAPTER ONE

Landslide
OR,
Mudslide

On November 8, 1972, newspaper headlines heralded a landslide victory for President Nixon. Slightly more than a week later, smaller streamers announced that Big Sur in California had been buried by mudslides.

The newspapers may have confused the two events. Surely it would have been more accurate to announce that Richard Nixon was the beneficiary of a mudslide! Dizzy Dean—and no more apt person could have been chosen for the task, considering the president's predilections and attributes—could have signaled to all that Nixon "had slud on mud" into his second term.

At first peep (and by now many of us may have mustered up enough courage to do only that), any badmouthing of Nixon's almost clean sweep would seem to epitomize sour grapes. He won big, didn't he? Let's recap! Nixon won:

- over 60 percent of the popular vote

11

- every state but Washington, D.C., and Massachusetts
- 75 percent of the upper-income vote, 65 percent of the middle-income vote, and even 38 percent of the low-income vote
- traditionally secure Democratic supporters—57 percent of the Italians, 37 percent (some insist 43 percent) of the Jews, and even 11 percent of the blacks
- 65 percent of the voters over the age of 18 and 48 percent of those under 25 (although in the flush of victory he claimed the majority of the youth)
- 50 percent of the blue-collar industrial workers (compared to only 33 percent in 1968)
- the South, the North, the East, and the West (and that's about all there is)
- almost all the support Wallace had in 1968 while gaining in groups hostile to George

That kind of victory is hard to argue with, isn't it?—NO!!!

Dorothy Parker's trenchant comment fits perfectly the re-election of Richard Nixon—"There is much less here than meets the eye."

Let's look again at the figures: fewer than 46 million people voted for Richard Nixon. That is only 2½ million more people than voted for Lyndon Johnson eight years before when there were far fewer people and only persons over age 21 could vote. In fact, despite a potential increase of over 25 million voters, less than 5 million more people voted in 1972 than in 1964.

The lack of voter activity is only one indication of the tenuous nature of the Nixon victory. There is yet another indicative clue: he carried *no one* with him; he brought *no* enemies down to defeat. Even then National Republican Committee Chairman Senator Dole missed the significance of the whole thing when he lamented that, while it was a personal victory for the president, it was no victory for the Republican party. It *certainly* was no Republican victory. The party lost 2 more seats in the Senate, falling to a deficit of 14 votes, and yet another governor, thus finding themselves outnumbered in the state houses by a 31-to-19 count (while just four short years ago two thirds of the governors were Republican).

Dole is wrong in that it wasn't even a personal victory for President Nixon. He had not, as one of Nixon's gushing supporters claimed (*Life* magazine, November 17, 1972), "achieved a philosophical identity with some deep American values." To the contrary, what the election revealed was that in 1972 America had lost its values, and *how* this happened is the story that needs desperately to be told.

TV commentators, bored with themselves and the election, tried desperately to generate some excitement on the most tensionless of all election nights. The one issue they fretted over was the absence of a coattail effect. The discussion wasn't too profound: on the one hand, they tended to argue that presidents don't generally carry with them too many other candidates (Johnson gained *only* 37 congressional supporters as a result of his victory); or they took the tack that Nixon didn't try to win congressional seats (that was the essence of Dole's comments). Both arguments are nonsense. And, while no precocious or perceptive child was able to escape the secret service men long enough to announce that the emperor was naked, it should be obvious that Nixon was not able to generate a coattail effect—*not* because no one ever does, or because he sat on them, *but* because he never had any coattails for anyone to hang onto. The 37 congressional seats President Johnson gained *were* significant. Prominent opponents of his regime fell and his prominent supporters survived. Not so in 1972. Not *one* highly vocal anti-Nixon incumbent lost his seat and a considerable number of important pro-Nixon supporters bit the dust. That doesn't happen often even in close elections. It is time, then, to get to what really happened in the presidential election of *1972.*

Nineteen seventy-two marked the end of the American Dream! In 1972 the public lost a vision that America could establish "liberty and justice for all." Nineteen seventy-two was a resignation, not an affirmation. It was a declaration that the United States was forsaking its vision of livable cities, happy children, secure old age, harmony among nations. The electorate chose instead to close off debate. The 60 percent of the population voting for Nixon expressed a weariness of critics of America who offered no believable solution to the problems at hand. Because there was no projection of a happier future, no promise of surcease of acrimony and complaint and because there was no projected place in the sun to go, the election amounted to a paraphrase of the Talmud, "If you don't know where you are going, anyone can lead you there." So much for blanket assertions—the time has come to build a case.

Nixon's mudslide stemmed from an erosion of political consciousness and understanding on the part of the electorate. Four factors contributed to this erosion. (1) The lack of any form of political education. Neither media nor schools prepared anyone for complex decision making. To the contrary, mass media (and even restricted elitist media) offered neither analysis of current problems nor proposals suggesting ways to go. (2) McGovern as candidate failed to develop understanding through either his posture or his platform. (3) The forward movements of the sixties—the anti-war, civil rights, antipoverty, ecological sanity mobilizations became liabilities rather than assets in the development of political awareness among the broadest segments of the electorate. (4) The emergence of a group of "new realists," a renowned group of scholars who proclaimed that real changes in the United States were impossible, arguing that we must

14

scale down our aspirations to less laudable goals and that persons persisting in dreaming big dreams were at the very least suspect in their scholarship and intelligence.

Presidential elections make sense and can be legitimately characterized as landslides if one candidate wins big and the electorate knows what they voted for. A mudslide occurs when opponents to the candidate slip and slide and are unable to gain footholds. If the voter is to be knowledgeable, he must have developed a background in political thinking and must have information; otherwise, his vote is pure caprice and results are more a factor of carnival than political consciousness. As societies become more complex, the information required for intelligent decision making increases quantitatively and qualitatively. An intelligent vote for president presumes sophistication about economics, ecology, engineering, logistics, organizational structure, human potentialities, geopolitics, and so on. An enlightened electorate is a prerequisite for any claim to landslide victory. None of our informational or educational institutions offered much in these areas.

The schools, in their fundamental obligation to prepare youth for citizenship, have failed completely.* Schools continue to be places, as Jules Henry charged years ago, where children go to learn how to become stupid about war, economics, labor, minorities, poverty, and communism. Inasmuch as the presidential election deeply involved all of these issues, Nixon, in his victory, is more to be pitied than congratulated. Schools fail at even more basic levels—which has implication for political outcomes. Children never learn what large numbers mean—they find it difficult to distinguish between millions, billions, and trillions—many elementary school teach-

---

* For a more thorough exposition of the school deficiencies in this area, read Arthur Pearl, *The Atrocity of Education* (New York: Dutton, 1972).

ers have the same problem. Thus it is possible for a candidate to prate about economies leading to savings of *millions* of dollars in cutbacks in welfare benefits, school children lunches, or excesses in poverty programs while almost in the same breath he may ask for billions of dollars more (a billion is one thousand million) for military expenditures. Years ago, in a more simple world, this was known as being penny-wise and pound foolish and people understood it and voted accordingly.

The schools are not our only institutions derelict in political education. Television is undoubtedly the most culpable of all institutions. Everything in television is flip and slick— the focus is on description. The analysis, when it exists, is thin and banal and there is *no* prescription. It engages in yet another political miseducation. It enhances the "expert" status of political hacks on such shows as "Meet the Press" and "Face the Nation," where such functionaries as the secretary of defense would lay on the public, in very protective situations, a seemingly overwhelming array of facts and figures, conveying to the listener that the speaker alone has all the relevant information and that decisions in this area are beyond the capabilities of ordinary man.

Commentators on television, radio, and syndicated for newspapers are—almost without exception—shallow. They are content with gossip or, when really digging, unearth some fragments of information not tied together into a comprehensive analysis. Not *one* political commentator ventured a plan for America's future. Thus the public was given an extremely limited political education—limited in time, limited in scope, limited in vision.

The consequence of all this was reinforcement of the notion that the problems facing us are not soluble, that only a few experts know what's going on, that the sensitivity of the

16

issues means that the important information must remain classified, that challengers of this view are suspect and, if not downright unpatriotic, certainly not right in the head. Ring down the American Dream—ring up Clockwork Orange.

McGovern, as candidate, didn't instruct. He failed to present in sharp contrast the difference in priorities and programs. The advertised difference, proclaimed by Nixon in his nomination acceptance speech, "At long last the American people would have a clear choice in philosophies," didn't materialize. When the election was over, McGovern's philosophy remained as unclear as Nixon's. The McGovern campaign failed not because of its vote (and that vote was catastrophic—McGovern's vote was barely a million more than Goldwater's 1968 total) ; the campaign failed because it never clarified issues—in the end, it confused rather then educated.

But now comes a critical failure. In a sense, the election signaled *taps* for the peace movement, the ecology movement, the antipoverty movement, and the racism movement, *as they were constituted* in the sixties. It must be understood that Nixon didn't shoot down these movements—they died of congenital defects. And, in fact, what Nixon amounted to was the mighty hunter who, seeing it already dead, rested his foot on the mammoth's head and called for the photographers.

How was the peace movement flawed? It wasn't instructive. It started out as an effort to educate in the teach-ins of 1965 and degenerated to the mill-ins in 1972. Even the instructive phase faltered—its initial thrust was to focus on the warlike intentions of the U.S. government. It never graduated into proposals for peace. To the contrary, in many instances it became more wrapped up in championing the opponent's cause (a support, incidentally, never requested by the Viet Cong or the North Vietnamese) rather than in laying forth a set of specific steps the United States must take for peace.

Thus, because of lack of vision, a needed movement lost steam, reducing itself to sectarian quibblings until ultimately it was captured by Richard Nixon himself.

The basic flaw of the racial equality movement was that it tried to instill guilt in the white majority. History is the chronicle of human oppression. Historical wrongs are never undone. Racial equality is a vision of the *future* and will come only when strategies involving work, urban development, health care, tax reform, schooling, and so on are thought through and enunciated to ensure that a fairer share of economic wealth, political power, and quality of life is available to nonwhites in the United States. Rhetoric of anger, hate, and dire threats of destruction replaced specific plans for change. The movement was based on fear, not hope.

The poverty program came a cropper because it was based on the notion that the nation could have its cake and eat it too. The economic thought underlying all programs designed to help the poor was based on a growing economy which would add significantly to the wealth of the super rich. Apart from some incendiary language of "maximum feasible partic-ipation of the poor," which led to some painful consequences for the poor trying to practice what the U.S. government preached, very little happened to poor people during the pov-erty war. The amount of money appropriated to fight poverty was insignificant (the poverty programs amounted to much less money than that given to rich farmers *not* to grow food) and even those limited funds rarely found their way into the hands of the impoverished. The attack on the program became very good politics and, while scandal could be found (never on the scale that plagued the military), the principal issue of inadequate funding and inappropriate theory was never adequately discussed in those circles where big deci-sions are made. In the end, the rich kept their riches and what the poor were forced to eat was hardly cake.

The ecology movement was victimized by its doomsday mentality. The environmental populists, particularly Paul Ehrlich, arrived as latter-day religious prophets, screaming to one and all to repent before it was too late. In time, the over-statement of a case became black humor—a camp horror show called "Let All the People Die" in which Bette Davis could have played Paul Ehrlich and Joan Crawford, Barry Commoner. This is the stuff that titillates, but it never generates effective movements.

The major movements of the sixties were damaged in other ways besides their reliance on fear and morality. They didn't interconnect. Rightfully, those concerned with poverty and racism perceived the environmentalists as at best a diversion—at worst, a threat. It isn't a long jump from suggestions of voluntary birth control procedures for underdeveloped countries, to insistence on sterilization as prerequisite for welfare benefits, to—genocide!

Even such obviously related tragedies as racism and poverty were analyzed in isolation. There can be no solution to race, class, sex, or ethnic injustice in the United States unless there are enough (1) jobs for all and (2) desirable jobs for all. Whenever there is not enough work, and especially when there is not enough good work, somebody has to be left out —these will be people without power or connections. Maybe because such a relationship *is* so obvious it continues to be overlooked.

War relates to poverty. Monies spent on pursuing or pre-paring for war cannot be spent on removing blight, developing health care, paying salaries for teachers, or constructing day care centers for the very young or the very old.

There were yet other serious deficiencies in the efforts to politicize the population in the sixties. The movements were alien from the populations they sought to lead: the language, tempo, mood, and temperament were foreign. They were somber—and humorless—and thus the people left them for more enjoyable activities. There can be no more devastating criticism than that, compared to the doomsday ecologist, the ranting peacemonger, the self-righteous civil rightist, the objurgating defender of the poor—even Richard Nixon looked good.

That the efforts to correct the century-old enigmas and disorders fell on hard times, that they fragmented, is lamentable, that Richard Nixon was a beneficiary of these difficulties is also unfortunate. But it would be an act of irresponsibility to leave even an introductory statement with only a description of the shortcomings. That *something* was tried in the sixties was in itself important and from those trials much is to be learned. Despite overwhelming odds and lack of preparedness, experiments succeeded: supposedly seriously retarded minority children learned what experts decreed was impossible for them; admissions policies to universities were changed; persons at the total mercy of usurers obtained legal counsel. There is another important body of knowledge to be obtained from the sixties—we learned what *not* to do! And, if we take seriously Wendell Phillips's counsel that there is no defeat, but only education, the movements of the sixties provided all of us, participants and observers, with an excellent education.

The American Dream did not die because of mere or benign neglect, or because of bungling or overzealousness on the part of the dreamers. A significant role was played by the dream killers. These were well-situated intellectuals anointed with that balm secreted in the vaults of the most exalted universities. From these stations this group of "realists" did a job with surgical skill. They slithered and oozed their way into the public consciousness (partially because they said things the public wanted so much to hear)—they announced that, perhaps, blacks *were* inferior to whites; that perhaps poverty *couldn't* be solved; that perhaps *full* employment was economically unfeasible; that perhaps, regardless of what happened in schools, life conditions of the poor would be unaffected; that perhaps man was so much a part of the technical world that human dignity or liberty was no longer possible. These groups of scholars were "liberals," mind you, and they laid much of the blame for the cacophony and destruction of the sixties on the "naive environmentalists" who encouraged the dreamers and in some instances even formulated new dreams. The dream killers call themselves scientists; we encounter them throughout this book. We do not acknowledge their claim. They are scientistic, they use the techniques and the language of science but go no further. True scientists have always been visionaries; vision killers don't qualify. Vision killers had import because they were "true believers"; they, like all human beings, drew from their experiences, their needs, and their group supports to present their notions as unassailable truth. This added to the impact of their words.

A true political education is dynamic. What happens in any category or sector affects all others. An exciting candidate affects social study activity even with the most abstruse teacher. A vibrant civil rights movement forces even the most superficial political hack to respond or retire. A coordinated educational program stimulates a public to demand from its electoral process answers where empty phrases reign supreme. Intellectuals articulating new visions clearly enough so that the less well schooled can understand do turn voters on, just as intellectuals can throw cold water on persons who want to venture forth. Nineteen seventy-two degenerated into a mudslide because the necessary elements for political growth were either missing altogether or were just not developed enough.

The issues of peace, poverty, racism, and an ecological society remain with us; how they can be developed into programs which elect presidents needs to be understood. First, however, we must understand how and why Richard Nixon was able to either parry thrusts against him or turn them to his advantage. To do this, we must discuss voting as a psychological process.

Robert Southey, an otherwise undistinguished British poet, might have summarized in his one remembered poem Richard Nixon's election triumph:

> "What good came of it at last?"
> quoth little Peterkin.
> "That I cannot tell," said he,
> "But 'twas a famous victory."

CHAPTER TWO

Voting as a psychological phenomenon
   OR,
How an oleaginous blob becomes
perfectly clear

There doesn't seem much indication that the 46 million
people who voted for Richard Nixon had any reasonable idea
what they were doing or, to put it more precisely, very few of
them even voted for the same person. The election was a
grabbag in which everybody paid the same price, put a hand
into a receptacle, got a prize, and called it Richard Nixon.
One perfectly clear indication of voters' confusion is a lack of
pattern in the voting. Otherwise, why would there be a dole-
ful Dole? Why would a conservative *National Review* lament
that "the 93rd will still be a Democratic Congress and so far as
any change in the ideological balance was indicated by the
shift in membership, it may be a degree or two left of the
92nd" (November 24, 1972, p. 1286). Why would women
have gained substantially in the House and lost their single
representative in the Senate? Why would a right centrist president be elected by the same voters who sent 80 new faces to

Congress—"and the new mix is younger, more volatile, far less manageable than its established leadership" (*Newsweek*, November 13, 1972, p. 38).

Another indication of voters' confusion was their own reports and the reports of expert analysts. From every quarter there was befuddlement about the presidential election. Some blamed the whole thing on McGovern—"Democrats torn from their normal allegiance by one main issue—the shortcomings of their party's candidate" (*Newsweek*, November 13, 1972, p. 30).

Columnist Harriet Van Horne attributed the election to people voting "their fears, their pitiful hopes and their meanest prejudices" (*New York Post*, November 8, 1972).

The *National Review*, from the right, describes the presidential popular vote landslide as "meaningless," "forged in no considerable part by the negative dynamism of anti-McGovernism" (*New York Review of Books*, November 24, 1972) (which was something different than just the weaknesses of McGovern the man).

Meanwhile, socialist Michael Harrington attributed Nixon's victory to those myths about the United States believed by the voter: that the United States has been throwing away large sums of money on social problems—that a wide-scale governmental permissiveness favored criminals and welfare recipients and that the dearth of leadership in the United States was a direct result of government-inspired dependency (*The Nation*, November 27, 1972).

Neither expert nor tyro could agree on what accounted for this overwhelming victory. In fact, it was entirely possible that no *two* people with their identical vote pictured in their mind's eye a leader who would act the same way toward peace, domestic tranquillity, employment, taxes, special favors to big business, special favors to the factory worker, law enforcement, environmental protection, inflation, support for

24

the mentally retarded, minorities, education, welfare, health services, city renewal, mass transportation, international relations, and so on. In other words, a lot of people got fooled in 1972.

But that should come as no surprise. Fooling people is woven into the very fabric of American life. Everybody does it. Sometimes it is the most innocent of fun—other times, it's the basis of malice and mayhem. Con men make their living on the willingness of persons to be fooled. Lonely housewives spend weeks planning a surprise birthday to pleasantly fool their husbands, and husbands spend just about as long fooling their wives into believing that they were fooled. Girls get fooled into pregnancy, boys into marriage. Without fooling, television wouldn't exist. Parents try to fool children about lots of things—particularly about how well they are getting along. Children learn to fool parents. District attorneys fool juries and innocent people go to jail; defense attorneys fool juries and guilty people go free. Ministers fool congregations. Undercover narcotics agents fool unsuspecting addicts. And so it goes, and all this relates to how presidents get elected.

Fooling is an interesting psychological process. It involves both victims and victimizers. There is suspense and doubt in the process and that is why Abraham Lincoln commented that it didn't always happen, and for some few it never happens at all. Fooling involves a learning process, a motivational process, and a perceptual process. People learn to be fooled; they want, and sometimes even need, to be fooled; and they see things that others don't see for the fooling to take place. The 1972 election is partially to be explained by the learning received by the electorate. Learning has a very specific meaning. It is the change of behavior which recurs as a result of experience. Thus humans learn to walk, talk, read, play tennis or chess, or they learn the logistics of the city in which they live, to memorize their and other people's telephone numbers, to subscribe to religious beliefs, and to vote for the candidate of their choice. Learning is still a rather mysterious process. Psychologists are divided among many different theories. Some regard learning as a rather passive process. The learner modifies behavior when that behavior is regularly rewarded and unlearns or extinguishes behavior when it is either ignored or punished. Other theories place more importance on active selecting and thinking of the learner. (The author subscribes to this latter view.)

The reelection of Richard Nixon is easily explained by *any* learning theory. It is certainly a logical consequence of mechanistic behaviorism (the learner as passive responder to rewards or punishments). According to such theory, the electorate learned to vote for Richard Nixon the same way that children learn to talk.

> A child learns to speak when he makes sounds that parents want to hear and they pat the child on the head or give it cookies or smile at it whenever it produces or comes close to producing the desired sound.

Such a theory explains undesirable behavior as well. For example, drug addiction can be explained as behavior learned through a system of appropriate rewards. A youngster learns that he or she receives a pleasurable physiological reaction after the ingestion of a drug. Attempts at rehabilitation of the addict are often governed by the same theory: that is, unpleasant experiences (prison) will inevitably accompany drug use. Both drug use and drug abstinence often rely on social reinforcers—friends and associates who either encourage or discourage the use. Now look to the application of such a theory to presidential elections. What are the rewards and punishments for such behavior? When the stimulus is clear—that is, if one candidate promises to reward only the rich and the other candidate promises to reward only the poor—then the election is a classical operant conditioning problem and can be explained by two levers and two different classes of pigeons: one dark, the other light. If every time the light-colored pigeon pushes the lever on the right he gets food, and if every time he pushes down the lever on the left he gets nothing, it will not take too long for the pigeon to learn the problem and soon he will push only the right lever. If a problem is just the opposite for dark-feathered pigeons, they too will learn to solve it. And if you place a picture of Richard Nixon over the lever to the right and a picture of George McGovern over the lever to the left, and if 46 white pigeons and 30 dark pigeons participate in the experiment, in a very short while, on every try, the Nixon lever will receive 60 percent of the votes (not exactly, but pretty close—and that kookie pigeon or two who can't learn his left from his right is likely to be served as an out-of-the-ordinary dinner treat). That's all well and good for the classical experiment.

But how about the 46 million pigeons—whoops! humans—who actually voted for Mr. Nixon. What rewards did they get? Obviously, the rewards and punishments associated with the presidential election are not the same the pigeons received in psychological experiments. People rewards were promises, but nonetheless they were there. And what were the rewards promised for voting for Richard Nixon? Well, they were peace, employment, safe streets, a dollar which buys something, status in the family of nations, a stable dependable courageous leader, and reduced taxes.

These are pellets for which any pigeon would be glad to vote. Now, however, comes some of the rub. Let's go back to the pigeons in their cages. They had lots of experience in learning the problem. Every time they voted wrong, they got immediate feedback. This isn't what happens in a presidential campaign. You get only one chance. But, in all of those promises of rewards, the voter did have some feedback or some information. Mr. Nixon was the incumbent. A good number of pigeons had pushed those levers before and for the very same things—but hadn't received them as yet. So what had they learned? Well, for one thing, the problem as framed isn't exactly as the election was. Let's return to those pigeons in the cages, only now, every time those white pigeons press the right lever they get a slight shock and some pretty crumby-tasting food, and every time they press the wrong lever they get sometimes the same food but more often much less palatable food and the same or more intense shock. And the reverse holds true for the dark pigeons. Then you can expect some changes in behavior from the original experience. For one thing, some pigeons just aren't going to vote. And that makes it a lot closer to what happened in the 1972 election. When you interview them afterward, they will say something like this (in "pigeon English"—ugh!) : "Well, I tell you, the guy I voted for wasn't much, but the other guy, I just couldn't go for; couldn't trust him, you know, didn't know what I was getting into."

Well, that's closer to what the election was all about. But it's still too simple. Both the experiment is too simple and the learning theory is too simple. It is, however, an extremely important learning theory to know. It is a theory on which the Nixon campaign was based. It is the notion of learning that has captured a great many educationists who base much of reading instruction on programming visual stimulus and close association with sound and rewarding the child with praise, tokens, candy, and even money for the correct response. The identical learning theory is applied to fooling people in elections.

It is based on the thought processes of B. F. Skinner and is known as operant conditioning or behavior modification (so named because the animal or human does something first and is either encouraged or discouraged after by persons controlling the reward systems). The basic tenet of the theory is that people can be programmed by strategic application of rewards and punishments. Most of the public relations firms which manage election campaigns by programming, packaging, and merchandising candidates are devoted to the belief that a mindless, passive electorate can be persuaded to vote in precisely the same way a passive population can be persuaded to buy soap or corn flakes. In *The Selling of the President* such a view is graphically presented. The public is seen as a group of persons who can be influenced by promises of rewards or, conversely, by presentation of a candidate having the attributes that they already like.

The theory of the mindless electorate is consistent with H. L. Mencken's comments that nobody ever starved to death insulting the intelligence of the American people. It is *not* the view espoused in this work. To the contrary, the voter is presented as an intelligent human being and his apparent foolishness is a reflection of limited knowledge, limited options, and limited visions available to him. The voter appears mechanistic or stupid because he or she has had so little knowledge of and experience with political matters, particularly at the level of the presidency. Where can he or she learn about the presidency? One, from the presidential candidates themselves; two, from formal schooling experience; three, from other educative media—magazines, books, radio, newspapers, television; four, from family, friends, colleagues, union members, church members, fellow Kiwanians; five, from formal political organizations which search them out and give them information—and that's about it.

Learning about the presidency, particularly if one argues from a view of man as a thinking organism, is further complicated by the amount and kind of knowledge that a voter must have if his or her vote is to indicate a reflective, intelligent decision. The voter must know about the duties of the presidency, the kinds of persons who should serve, the real personalities of the candidates. The voter must have a sound base in economics, ecology, political science, organizational theory, and so on to evaluate whether a presidential decision in any particular area is wise or unwise. The fooling of the voter in specific instances—peace, employment, health, environment, welfare, youth, minorities, inflation—is treated later in considerable depth in separate chapters. But, first, let's touch briefly on two general themes which make intelligent people act like fools.

Learning to be fooled in presidential elections stems from a great many different experiences. Some of the setting up takes place very early in the formal educational process. In early school years, children learn that only "great men" become presidents—people who never tell lies, and who emancipate slaves, win important battles, and cure depressions. And, in fact, if the president didn't do anything great, he will not even get studied.

Children and adults learn that presidents, in addition to being wise and good, must make decisions transcending common competence. This of course follows—great men wouldn't bother with mundane matters and, conversely, difficult problems require a genius for solution.

Learning about presidents is vicarious and remote. Very few of us have any direct experience with presidents—we don't interact with them or match wits with them (except we few critics who generally have imaginary debates with them on such issues as welfare and tax reform, and then the presidents do become mere mortals indeed because we win every time). Thus all learning is dependent on secondary sources —reporters, commentators, historians, secretaries—and as such tends to be dry, lifeless, and incomplete.

The president's personal presence must be remote—there is no way that one person could be on intimate relations with

200 million people (even Henry Kissinger hasn't been accused of such vitality). But, in another much less defensible way, the presidency is distant and foreign and that is in our universal ignorance of his duties. We know vaguely that he is checked and balanced by the courts and Congress; we know that he signs important papers, appoints people to important posts, entertains important visitors (or is entertained by them), and makes important speeches—but that's about as far as it goes. What we learn about the president is supported from all sides. It is reinforced (to use some of the jargon of mechanistic learning theorists) by parents, peers, policemen, and politicians themselves.

The deification of the president, the exaltation of the office, and the remoteness of the experience are one set of learnings setting up most of the voters to be fooled most of the time. This kind of learning offends thinking people. It sets up a kind of dissonance; it just doesn't fit. There are lots of ways of dealing with dissonance. One way is to close off thinking about the matter, to drive it out of your mind, to think of other things—Raquel Welch, bridge clubs, the 49ers and so on. Another way is to discount the learning you have received before—hedge on your bets, as it were. And, of course, both learning to tune out or to distrust your information contributes to the foolishness of potential voters. (This reaction against overstatement is found everywhere and provides a reasonably good argument against man being merely a passive learner.) This is a learning that leads to cynicism. The cynics or debunkers gain from their experiences the knowledge that they are too smart to be fooled; they know better; they know that presidents weren't too much, that they lied, messed around with women not their wives, conspired in shady deals, never freed slaves, and so on.

Cynics have discovered other things because of their experiences in political campaigns. They know that the outcomes are fixed because the candidates they worked for lost. They know that whatever Big Money wants, Big Money gets (and that includes Lola) and, since they can bring considerable data and logic to bear which seemingly support their views, they become a group ready to be fooled.

There is the obverse side of learning that contributes to being fooled in presidential elections: forgetting. This is a process whereby human beings set aside their past experiences. Like learning, forgetting is logical and lawful. Forgetting can be explained as a result of the lack of rewards for behavior or as a function of a more active thought process. In either instance, it is related to reminding, to some external source which brings to the attention of the organism—in this case, the voter—aspects of candidate behavior. Thus it was that some voters were reminded that George McGovern changed his mind about such things as amnesty, welfare, and marijuana by an organized group of Democrats for Nixon. Much less effort was made to get the public to remember Richard Nixon's swivel-hipped political career (a factor touched on again later in this work). The key point, however, is that selective forgetting is obviously a crucial factor in any political campaign.

Motivation is extremely important in the election process. Learning and perception (seeing, tasting, feeling, hearing) are influenced by desires one wants and needs. Every human decision involves what I call "a phenomenological cost-benefit analysis." This means individuals weigh the plusses or minuses of everything they do from their own private perspectives. If the activity seems to have more good to it than bad, they do it, and if the reverse applies, they don't do it. This is almost always a conscious process. It appears mysterious and strange only because it is difficult for anyone to really understand what is important to someone else. Most psychologists readily accept the notion of needs. They recog-

32

nize that human behavior is lawful. People do things for reasons. Abraham Maslow, the late eminent humanist psychologist, suggests a hierarchy of needs. Highest priority must be given to matters of survival (food, shelter), then to other vital needs (immediate security and safety), and, only after such basic matters are attended to, can humans turn to more lofty concerns. Maslow calls the most noble level of human attainment "self-actualization." I argue that all behavior reflect a human desire to attain fulfillment of security, comfort, belonging, usefulness, competence, and meaning in one's existence. Robert White, the Harvard psychologist, for example, argues that the need for mastery over something is a very important element in personality development. The noted existentialist Viktor Frankl insists that humans have an insatiable desire to make their lives meaningful. All this applies in the fooling that goes on in politics.

Motivation affects political activity at two very distinct levels and one is the gratification coming from a sense of involvement in the campaign: the joy of accomplishment, the camaraderie with fellow supporters, the sense of importance to others who are with you in this venture. There is yet another gratification coming from politics, the fulfillments offered by the leader—the security he brings you, the potential comforts, the reestablishment of community. Both levels of motivation make political fooling not only possible but in most instances probable and, in some instances, necessary for the voter's emotional security.

Fooling comes easiest when there is a low level of interest and participation. Commentator after commentator observed the marked lack of interest in the 1972 presidential campaign. One reason was the lack of motivation at the level of citizen participation. It isn't easy for many people to feel secure, comfortable, among friends, useful, or masterful doing things in a political campaign, particularly at the presidential level; things are just not organized that way. It is curious that on those rare occasions when a group of grass rooters put their enthusiasm to work and get their candidate through the primary, in the process generating a real sense of community, they are replaced by the "pros" or "pols" who reorganize the campaign on efficient, cold, and inhuman lines. Computer runs are requested to single out "swing" precincts. Public opinion surveys are purchased to get a "fix on where our candidate is" and thus they learn that "he must play down his abortion stand, reinterpret his stand against military spending, soften up his views on law and order in the black community, reassert his opposition to restrictive gun laws to the sportsman, and so on, to make sure that he isn't just a one-issue candidate." In such a campaign, the "pols" scientifically determine the response to fund-raising letters and ensure that a meeting with Colonel Smith Jones, President of Consolidated Portholes, is arranged since he gave big in the 1968 campaign. And thus the friendly "Mom and Pop country store" type of campaign is replaced by a supermarket and all the workers in the campaign lose their status and become mere checkout clerks, only less so. The bigger and more important the campaign, the more difficult it is for workers to gain a sense of true community and that is a paradox which persons concerned with participatory democracy will have to put their minds to (something I attempt to do in this book).

The struggles for comfort and security often limit political participation. People are most secure with persons they know best, who are most like them. Thus the campaign often settles down into converting the already converted. Why ring doorbells of persons whom you know don't like you? Why not leave literature with persons in the opposite camp rather than engage them in debate? If they are to be engaged in a debate, attack them hard so your friends will know you are brave and strong rather than allow the possibility of the other guy making points. For comfort and security, the headquarters are staffed by people who not only like each other but who did similar things in 1964–1966–1968–1970. (That most of those were losing campaigns seems forgotten.) The more the campaign seems to be a bummer, the stronger the need to retreat to a friendly sanctuary. Thus even the most political groups hang on because at least among themselves they have companionship and security of trusting relationships while outside they are absolutely alone.

As campaigns become more "scientific" (I prefer the term "scientistic"), as they are run on sound management principles, the same sorts of feelings of insignificance that affect workers in big corporations affect workers' feelings about political work. They can no longer generate a sense of usefulness or competence. The average, ordinary campaign worker doesn't raise money, he licks envelopes—no, he doesn't, a machine does that! The average, ordinary worker doesn't explain the issues carefully; field-tested campaign literature does that. He does some advance work for the rallies when the candidate or some of his big-name buddies try to rouse votes or raise money, but those involvements are minimal; only a small number of persons are involved and even those aren't able to get too much from their involvement. This we have come to call "progress" (much as we call the development of nuclear weaponry progress). I don't see much hope for the future of democracy if we continue along such a path.

In the absence of gratification in election participation, particularly participation in an underdog campaign, the attributes inspired by the leader become increasingly important. The leader must provide some promise of personal fulfillments to win his election. The presidential candidate becomes a figure understood only against the backdrop of a general climate or set of expectations. Gestalt psychologists have explained the changing of the perception of a visual stimulus as a background is altered. Something similar occurs in politics. The political figure is perceived differently in different contexts. In times of intense optimism, people expect grand visions from their president; in times of resignation, people expect stolidness and stability from their president. The situation isn't static; some exceptional campaigns can change the entire temper of a people and some dullards can dampen a people ready to be enthused. But the principle applies, and this is especially true of 1972. For reasons hinted at previously, and to be elaborated on later, this was no year for big visions. No impossible dreams in 1972—no pointed-headed idealists, if you please, just a plumber who can fix the stopped-up toilet, thank you.

The lack of grandiosity in the public mind means that expectations from their leaders are scaled down accordingly. In fact, the hope is that the leader won't allow what little they have now to deteriorate further. Thus they retreat to the position of the treed hunter who calls on his Lord only for this: "If you can't help me, don't help the bear!"

For security, they want to maintain their jobs, protect their country from enemies (more imagined than real), keep their property from rampaging criminals on the street (that threat becomes less imaginary every day), and envision some prospect of an enjoyable old age.

For comfort, they want what little luxuries they now possess and which some see the ecologists as trying to steal from them.

For belonging, they want their bridge clubs, fraternities, football teams (on which they vicariously star every Sunday), and neighborhoods, which are seemingly denied them by crusaders and nonwhite-lovers of suspect patriotism.

For competence, they want appreciation of the things they do, somehow being undermined by technical processes beyond their understanding.

36

For usefulness, they want an opportunity to work, to function in their community, to receive appreciation from their children and others with whom they have been associated by work, neighborhood, nationality, religion, or friendship.

For meaning, they want a world that makes some sense; they want problems which can be controlled, if not solved, a reassurance that those at the helm of the ship of state are persons well rooted in reality. In these times they want a fairy captain who knows where Hoboken or Tiburon is rather than some crazy who is going to drop us off the edge of the earth.

The factors that lead to perceived status of any one candidate come from a learning about the political process they have received, from the competition, the perceived qualities of the opponent or opponents, and from the background furor of political activity going on and around the candidates. Giving these as the important factors, perhaps now the perception of Richard Nixon as a desirable leader from so many diverse perspectives becomes slightly less puzzling.

Some saw him, from their very private concerns, as a source of security, comfort, usefulness, competence, and belonging. Others saw him as less a threat to security than his opponent. This is a very important consideration. Social psychologists Muzafer Sherif and Carl Hovland have demonstrated "that the latitudes of rejection" are more important in political decision making than "the latitudes of acceptance." That is, people have a much easier time in agreeing on what they don't like than they do on what they do like. Thus, as some have already argued, Richard Nixon may be president merely because his opponent was rejected even more than he was.

The perception of a candidate that leads either to voting for or against him (or not voting at all) is a functional process. It stems from prior learning and personal desires. The question remains, What, specifically, did different people see in Richard Nixon, and what relationship did his perceived presence have on the pressing issues of our time? In answer to this question, we have to look at the factors that influence voters' behavior.

Voters need help to be fooled. In the first chapter, four general factors leading to the fooling were brushed over lightly. These were the failure of the schools, the losing candidate's campaign, the political movements of the 1960s, and the new breed of social scientists who, hiding behind the claim of objective truth, discount the possibilities of new and better worlds. Other foolish notions, contributing to the fooling of the voters, need to be examined. Some of these notions are that McGovern was too left for the American people, that the Democratic party must retreat to a more cautious middle, that Nixon was unbeatable because he represented in his views and policies a central position, and, probably the most dangerous of all, that somehow political change can come about with very little preparation. These notions must be discussed because obviously decisions about them could affect political campaigns for generations to come.

And 1976 is almost here!

CHAPTER THREE

Fooling as a function of foolishness
OR,
A rolling stone is a political force

Votes aren't conjured out of thin air. People vote according to ideas which have penetrated and taken hold. These ideas are not magical in their creation, they are synthesized out of the voters' experience. Every election is thus a way station, a termination of a battle in the unending struggle for control over human bodies and minds. Two important factors contribute to foolish voting. One is the nature of the ideas to which the citizen has been exposed; the other is his ability to do something with those ideas. Political ideas come to the voter from four directions. There is a potential forward pull, a call for new adventures, the dream of a world ahead clean, pure, and free of injustice or disease. There is a backward tug —a return to Arcadia based on a notion of a paradise that has been lost, mislaid, or stolen. There is the hold-'er-steady-as-she-goes, an inertia designed to keep the political body moving without change in speed or direction. And there are a

39

variety of forces sharing only one common feature—they don't relate to any of the above: they are the detractors from politics that influence political behavior, the dead weights that sit on political consciousness much like a heavy dinner defying digestion.

When these forces are out of balance, people have virtually no opportunity but to be fooled politically. In the first chapter, an argument was advanced that the election of Richard Nixon was a direct result of the breakdown in balance, the absence of understandable and acceptable new visions. Well, that election is over. It was the fog that crept in on cat's feet, a brief response from life's petty pace, created very little sound, certainly generated no fury, and signified nothing except that Richard Nixon was returned to his offices in Florida, California, and Washington, D.C.

Elections are periodic events. Political activity is different; it is continuous. Events that influence human thought go on every day and what happens in an election gives forth ideas about what's possible in future political activity. Every election is an expansion or contraction in the belief in human capabilities. Each election spurs or inhibits analysis and reflection. These thought processes, once projected into the market place, become in themselves dynamisms and shape the political activity of the future. What is accepted as truth by a large number of persons rearranges the forces acting on political thought and behavior.

In this sense, the reelection of Richard Nixon may turn out to be hardly more than a bad joke—a manifestation of the egregious bad taste of the American people. The postelection analysis may represent, however, true tragedy. Four themes emerge out of the election: These were: (1) McGovern was too far left for the American people; (2) McGovern was personally a terrible candidate; (3) Nixon profited by a wholesale rejection of New Frontierism and Great Societyism; and (4) Nixon was a political genius who played the American public like Isaac Stern plays a violin.

All of these themes act against the notion of the need for new visions. The most devastating idea is that McGovern was too radical. What this means is that even his limited visions weren't acceptable and that the only course left us is to retreat, stand pat, or drop out.

Because the notion of McGovern's leftism is so widespread and because barely a month after the election the Democratic party reflected a change in this direction by appointment of a new national chairman, let's examine this view in some detail. The votes were hardly in when it was authoritatively announced from almost all directions, both formally and informally, that the election results indicated a rejection of Democratic extremism: that McGovern was to Democrats what Goldwater had been to Republicans. A group crystallized calling itself the Committee for a Democratic Majority (CDM) and announced that it would act as a gyroscope to try to get the Democratic party back on course again. *Newsweek*, in its characteristic style, encapsulated the thrust and composition of this new group:

> Its letterhead was a small who's who of the Democratic center—an assemblage of writers (Ben Wattenberg, Norman Podhoretz, Midge Decter), professors (John Roche, Nathan Glazer), congressmen (Missouri's Richard Bolling, Michigan's James O'Hara), old Humphrey hands (Max Kampelman, William Connell) and moderate blacks (Bayard Rustin, Patricia Roberts Harris). What pulled them together was the common conviction that the 1972 election was, as one of them described it, "a referendum on the new politics"—and that the ballot results spelled "no" by a landslide.
>
> From the outset, CDM's plans were ambitious: its founders hoped to make it an effective pressure group on the Americans for Democratic Action model, with a large paid-up membership (at dues of $15 to $100), a network of state chapters and a real moderating voice in party affairs. "We're providing a rallying point for those who feel they

have been turned aside, crushed, left behind by the McGovern movement," said Miss Decter. "There are a lot of people out there feeling lost." CDM's pitch to them is not unlike Humphrey's or Henry M. Jackson's in the primaries—a strong national defense, a resolute stand for law and order, a straight liberal-labor line on economic issues. The coalition is not at all squeamish about catering to the Wallace voters—and Wallace himself—to win them back to the party (*Newsweek*, November 27, 1972, p. 25).

The '72 election was precisely what they had called for as a group. The winning candidate stood for everything they wanted. He now owned one of the forces acting on the public. He got his majority because the CDM and others like them gave a legitimacy to Richard Nixon by undermining the *legitimacy* of dreams and visions. They justify their position on the grounds of practicality. There's nothing practical about losing. The group just doesn't understand that the world passed them by. They want something that *thankfully* can no longer exist—an effective Democratic party that can contain both racists and minorities, warriors and peacemakers, exploiters and exploited. No necromancer can reforge that amalgam. What the CDM has are some perceptual learning and motivational problems. Perceptually, they see things that don't exist. Just as Gertrude Stein once said of Oakland that there is no there there, there is no middle between left and right in the Democratic party. There is a vortex to which people can be sucked advocating things that can't or shouldn't be. There is a group of people who share nothing, not even common "latitudes of rejection," and who are struggling to find some sense of belonging by being where no one else is, and they are so desperate they'll accept anybody as companions. They are all George Webbers trying to go home again.

Let's probe further into the nature of their foolishness, examining the nature of the landslide from *their* perspective.

Now here are people who are viewing the returns of the 1972 election from a traditional liberal perspective. And yet, from this point of view, it wasn't nearly as bad in 1972 as it was in 1968 when they, as individuals, had almost all the power. Remember, in 1972 and 1968 the results of the presidential election were identical—Richard Nixon won. In 1968 he beat their man, in 1972 he beat the lefties' candidate, but there were some very important differences. Pennsylvania Senator Joseph Clark, a true labor liberal, came crashing down in 1968—nothing like that happened in 1972. Wayne Morse, among his other immense talents also a stalwart for labor rights, lost in 1968—no incumbent with such credentials fell in 1972. To the contrary, 1972 showed "McGovernism" producing gains for moderate blacks and labor liberals in legislative contests. Besides selective forgetting, the loss of detail and the remembering of only those things that fit, the CDM has another perceptual problem; they see some things that don't exist. They see a viable labor movement, a liberal Jewish community, and a liberal academia—all liberal in the way they define liberality—advocating strong defense budgets, moderate change in tax reform, increase in unemployment benefits and social security, and so on. Let's look at these delusions.

The labor movement hasn't been liberal for a long time, primarily because its leadership is old-fashioned and without vitality. Every year organized labor exercises less influence because its primary actors remain the same. They end up as obstructionists. Devoid of new ideas for full employment, they end up attacking environmentalists who they fear would create large-scale unemployment and frustrating efforts at racial integration, because with jobs hard to get, opening up membership to racial minorities would lead to more unemployment among those now dominating the membership. These are very real problems which are addressed later on in this book. But the main point to emphasize here is that the labor movement as a total group has no liberal concepts and can attract only those who want to return to times when there was no concern for relationships between economic growth and the environment and when minorities knew that their place was not in white unions.

The Jewish community won't be a unified liberal force again until peace comes in the Near East, which won't happen until real peace comes to the Far East—and until there is a rapprochement between blacks and Jews. The latter is knotty because the competition for scarce scholarships and professional employment sets up a conflict similiar to that facing blue-collar labor. Again, without visions of enough for both blacks and Jews (something not coming from the centralists in the Democratic party), the prospect of such alliances looks bleak indeed.

As for liberal academia, it has shattered. The faculty has splintered into many factions. The large percentage of the university faculty are now and always have been Miniver Cheevys. "They too love the Medici although they've never seen one and they too would have sinned incessantly had they been one." This group is now even more entrenched in campus activity than before. Many faculty members are flawed radicals, activists with poorly defined visions, but nonetheless rejecting the labor liberal. And many faculty members are into things that have political influence, but only indirectly. The faculty the CDM wants to attract has eroded in numbers and aged in years. They won't win back too many converts because the ones that they do have don't like to debate; they'd rather huddle in cabals and write articles for magazines like *Commentary* or *Public Interest* which mostly take after visionaries, sometimes justifiably.

Before the Committee for a Democratic Majority and persons who think like them get carried away by their dyspeptic analogy, they ought to recollect (if their needs let them) that the chief beneficiary of the Goldwater debacle in 1964 was not the centrist like Rockefeller or Romney but the primary loyalist—Richard Nixon—who went everywhere he was asked to make speeches and raise money, which disgruntled Republicans complain is more than he did in 1972. If there's to be a comparable reaction among Democrats in 1976 as there was among Republicans in 1968, the obvious heir to the Democratic nomination is Ted Kennedy, who made himself as available in 1972 as Nixon did in 1964. However, it is not yet either necessary or desirable to announce Ted Kennedy as heir apparent even though the Harris Poll has already declared him a winner over Spiro Agnew by landslide proportions in 1976.

It should not be too difficult to recognize the members of the emerging Committee for a Democratic Majority. They are the previously-referred-to vision killers. They are the retreating liberals; they do not talk of full employment or racial equality, at least in our lifetime, or harmony among nations or air that can't be seen. They are most vicious in the matter of social equality where they are among the first to dredge up the notion that perhaps racial equality is unobtainable because the poor are genetically inferior or, if they're not ready to jump on that bandwagon, they "realistically" assess the cost of true equality in dollars, political realism, and social unrest, concluding that the price is too high.

Do not be deceived. The people who generated the Committee for a Democratic Majority and others like them have exercised and still do exercise influence in political matters. In many instances, they have been the primary architects of social policy. They have had far more pull than their accomplishments would warrant. Nathan Glazer, with his colleague Daniel Patrick Moynihan, is second only to Henry Kissinger as a university professor who not only had this president's ear but his predecessor's as well. It is not that the CDM are "pols" out in the cold, but they no longer call *all* the shots. Their needs for power and recognition and competence and belonging to *the* group are at stake. And they suffer as do many factory workers, académes, and even prizefighters now that they ain't what they once was.

If the Democratic party does turn back, even if it wins, it can achieve pyrrhic victories only. The turn must be forward. The turn must be toward innovative, exciting, adventurous approaches—for peace, for racial harmony, for relief of poverty, for ecological sanity. And, to attain these visions, new groups must be formed which also must collect dues and exercise influence, but the stress here must be and should be very clearly different from that recommended by the CDM.

It must be understood and recognized that McGovernism never got to that exalted state. It wasn't even an almost-ism. It started too late and it remained too thin—that's the lesson which must be learned from 1972. Rather than proclaiming the McGovern campaign a disaster and then doing everything possible to make it so, there is a solid basis for an optimistic evaluation of the McGovern campaign.

The 1972 presidential campaign should give cause for optimism—it shows how much can be done with so little effort. It does, however, pinpoint the failures and weaknesses of over-optimism. The lessons to learn are:

1. If there is to be a winning election in 1976, work had better begin now.
2. The priority issues need to be determined and tied together into an intelligible package.
3. Every issue must carry with it a plan of action, a logical statement of things to be done for change with a defense of that position in logic and evidence.
4. Political activity must be made pleasurable, providing participants with fulfillment of basic needs.

46

5. Activities must take many forms: preparation for political decision making must be introduced in the schools (the distinction between political education and political indoctrination is discussed in chapters to come); leaders seeking office must forge public opinion rather than accept dictation from it; new-formed political movements must emerge to act as propelling instructive forces; and the Dr. Panglosses, who insist that if we don't have the best of all possible worlds, we are well on the way to it, must be met in educative open debate on campuses, union halls, mass media, and, if necessary, at half time during pro football games (many more specifics on all of this later).

Some people want to blame everything that happened in 1972 on McGovern himself—that George done himself in all by his lonesome. That's an easy out and an unfair conclusion. The onus of failure must be shared among all who desire a forward surge; but McGovern did contribute significantly to political confusion and, since a chapter is devoted to reflection on McGovern the candidate (Chapter 8), the matter is tabled until then.

Probably more discouraging than the liberals' call for retreat in the Democratic party is the way persons from whom one would expect visions responded. Many were too stunned to come forth with much. Michael Harrington's comments in *The Nation* (November 27, 1972), however, reflect a pretty common set of conclusions of those regarding themselves as radicals. Michael Harrington, then leader of the Socialist party of the United States, has excellent credentials. His book *The Other America* had profound impact on American thought. The work rightly qualified him to be the Christopher Columbus of poverty. He discovered poverty in the United States during the 1960s when very few people except the poor knew it existed (in this way he is very similar to

Columbus who discovered America when very few but the American Indians knew it existed). It has been almost universally recognized that he is one of the really bright minds of America (the same is generally said of William F. Buckley, and it's a terrible thing to say about anybody).

Michael Harrington muses in a rather confused way about the Nixon victory. He calls the election the myth that was real and credits Nixon with ferreting out the inner sanctum shibboleths of the American people—the essence of which is that the American people believe that the United States is throwing away lots and lots of good money on worthless poor people, mostly Blacks, all of which is building up dependency on government and leading to the type of permissiveness that undermines character and condones welfare, drug use, homosexuality, and abortion. That's not too bad as description. Many people do hold to such views and Richard Nixon did exploit those beliefs. Where Harrington falls apart is in his analysis. He attributes the first half of the myth (throwing away of money) on previous Democratic administrations, and the last half of the myth on the people supporting McGovern (here he sounds almost like the liberals who formed themselves into the Committee for a Democratic Majority). He argues that people associated wasteful social programs with Lyndon Johnson's "farewell budget," which claimed enormous increases in dollars spent on social programs, and thus people turned to Nixon and his promises of economies in these areas.

Harrington, in presenting this view, studiously avoids (selectfully forgets?) the fact that Nixon and particularly Democrats for Nixon use the Johnson type rhetoric to a fare-theewell. Remember, it was Nixon who claimed that *he* was the first U.S. president since World War II to have a Health, Education, and Welfare budget higher than a defense budget. Thus, with this single claim, *he* became an advocate for social causes and a fighter for peace. As for McGovernites offending large blocs of voters by championing reform of laws restricting abortion, use of marijuana, homosexual relationships between consenting adults, and so on, which affronted the "white working class, particularly the Catholic working class," well, of course such activities offended white workers. But the point is, given the absence of any forward political thought in their church, their unions, their newspapers, their friends, or in any part of their lives—*anything* would offend them. What Harrington won't admit is that white Catholic workers would rather talk about marijuana than socialism. They would prefer, above all else, to talk about football and Nixon does that more, if not better, than almost anyone.

Harrington is way off base when he talks about the permissiveness of our society, which he attributes to a decline in the authority of family and church and the ascendency of the militaristic corporations. Nonsense! We don't live in a permissive society. Catholic white workers know that and that's what burns them up about welfare recipients and "hippies," because they believe that these two groups are getting what workers can't get. That might be a mite selfish, but it's perfectly understandable. Because Harrington doesn't understand the lack of tolerance in a technological society, he serves no useful purpose to the group he would like to lead to new visions—the group he calls the working class. But misunderstanding permissiveness isn't Michael Harrington's biggest problem.* Harrington just doesn't understand the basic flaws of the social programs of the sixties. Again, he is like Columbus; he is unable to do anything with his discovery. The programs of the sixties were basically bad programs. Nixon is absolutely correct in insisting that monies were misspent. Where he is extremely vulnerable, however, is that the

* For a further analysis of the rigidification of *A Technological Society*, see Jacques Ellul's book by that title.

money continues to be misspent, only more so. But he won't be caught up because he is ultimately protected. Only the "extremists" can argue with him that a person who works shouldn't make more money than a person who doesn't. Nixon resonates with the notion that the workers do all the work and the idle poor get all the gravy. Hell! Change only one word and you have a great socialist slogan—that's what's got to be dealt with. Examine briefly one of the "ideas" of the sixties—the notion that people *should* be given unearned money, a guaranteed income, a livable welfare benefit. Even Richard Nixon has a version of it, calling it "a family assistance plan." That Nixon should endorse a vision of income without work should come as no surprise since the idea is reactionary, was originally inspired by backward-lookers (ultraconservatives), is currently enjoyed only by the rich, and could be achieved readily by giving every poor child a rich father.

Proposals for income without work are stupid. They are stupid politically because they anger those who work. They are stupid economically because they are costly with little benefit derived from the expenditures. They are stupid psychologically because they do not provide gratification for the recipient. They are stupid ecologically because they do not address the unmet work needs of our society and fail to abide by a very basic ecological law that there-ain't-no-such-thing-as-a-free-lunch.

The only vision that can unify a large number of people is a reformation of work—creation of a work world where everybody can contribute—even the aged and the young. Harrington, in pursuing his own mythological beast, takes a whack at Nixon when he argues that most welfare beneficiaries are "composed of children and the aging people whom even Mr. Nixon has not yet proposed driving back into the labor market." That completely misses the mark. It is not that the young and old should be driven back to the labor market, the truth is that they and many others have been driven out of the labor market and therein lies the tragedy. The work world of tomorrow shouldn't be a return to sweat-shops—children breaking their backs in garment factories or losing their lungs in coal mines or old people forced into drudgery. The work world should allow everyone an opportunity to make a contribution (expanded considerably in our chapter on work). Meanwhile, because of the bankruptcy of the dreamers, welfare recipients are hounded and oppressed. They'll continue to be until visionaries come up with something better either than Harrington's trying to convince people that bundles of money were not misspent in the sixties or by suggesting in some vague way that the left advocates should somehow unite with the "working class."

There are many other flaws in the thinking of modern progressives: use of violence, narrowness of perspective, sloppiness of language, lack of attention to organization, tactics, and strategies, and so on. But the point is that unless there is serious reflection or if in the absence of new proposals careless analysis becomes characteristic, our troubles will only deepen.

The retreat to the center of the Democrats and the albatrosses worn as neck pieces by radicals are not the only factors likely to lead to a continued imbalance of pressures on American political thinking.

The dead weights get heavier.

Campus bookstores still feature *I Ching* and organic gardening. Sports entice one group, X-rated movies probably the same group:

How about an X-rated "football game" between naked, ample-busted, narrow-waisted women, all of whom have long and shapely legs, whose uniforms consist only of brass knuckles and similar implements guaranteed to draw blood.

51

Wow! That would probably be the greatest drawing card of all time and I wonder if the president would offer his advice to the coach and players of such a game when *they* play in the Super Bowl.

The deflections from meaningful political thought can be found on television, becoming more taken with technical efforts and less interested in analysis and debate or consisting of aimless late night conversations with Norman Mailer or ten-minute synopses of the world with Walter Cronkite. Deflection is found in slavish adoration of music groups, some of whom pretend political awareness by composing themes which denigrate political and economic institutions, thereby detracting from serious political thought and action. All these leave the people unprepared for future elections and, unless changed, will make elections little more than exercises in random selections.

Now to the last point, Nixon's influence on his own election and the masterful way he managed his success. Doesn't he offer a clue for the way to go for the future, and shouldn't every political party which aspires to victory emulate him? No! First, he didn't do very much right. He made many serious blunders, but no one was there to take advantage. Two, he's no champion campaigner. He won in 1972 because he did almost nothing. When he tried hard, as he did in 1960 and 1962, he lost. He almost lost in 1968 and there's no assurance that if George Wallace had been able to campaign in 1972 he or the other George, and not Nixon, would be hailed as the chief.

Assume only that Wallace would have doubled his 1968 vote in 1972—which would be a conservative estimate considering his pre-shooting primary success—and assume that 95% of that gain would have come from the Nixon total and, instead of a Nixon landslide, the results become:

52

Nixon	28 million
McGovern	27 million
Wallace	20 million

Many Republicans have expressed anger over Nixon's lack of support of some party potentates who were knocked out of their legislative seats. They might have been very lucky. They might have lost more if he had helped. Which brings us to Mr. Nixon—Superstar—himself.

CHAPTER FOUR

A new majority in every mirage
  OR,
Kissinger as Merlin, Sammy Davis, Jr.,
as the White Knight

Presidents are special. The world as a whole hasn't had too many that could possibly qualify, and the United States has had only thirty-seven. That's pretty limited experience and it means that the presidency represents unique leadership. In any form or of any group, leadership is not too well understood; suffice to say, it is a complex phenomenon. At the national level, leadership involves the actual attributes of the chief executive, the part real or contrived that the public is allowed to see, the dynamics of the problem at hand, the latitudes of choice within the system (again, real or imagined), and the actual or felt needs of the people.

To truly make sense of the election, all the attributes of leadership must be considered. Let's begin with the mood of the people. In the first chapter it was claimed that the election was not an affirmation of anything but, to the contrary, a rejection of everything. If we couldn't stop the world and get

55

off, we at least could slow it down with Richard Nixon. People were tired of demonstrations and noise, doom-sayers and nay-sayers, and all they wanted to do was to sigh "enough already!" In the second chapter it was argued that the voter found in Richard Nixon a greater sense of security and congruent thought, among other needs, than emanated from his possible alternatives. Some further elaboration on these two statements. Voters aren't masochists; they don't like to be tortured. The Marquis de Sade won elections in insane asylums only. And voters aren't crazy; they only appear crazy to losing candidates. Some rules govern voter behavior. Almost inevitably, if voters are given a set of problems which defy solution, for their own psychological stability, they'll either insist that the problems don't really exist or that they are being solved, or they are willing to be deflected away by nonproblems because these have readily available solutions. Thus, for example, there is either no such thing as racism or it's being solved or it's an invention of conspiratorial forces like communists who can be easily dispatched. That's where Mr. Nixon comes in. He served as a rallying point for such views and presented what he called data to support all these notions. That the facts are suspect is a matter dealt with later, but Nixon did generate the aura of a man in control and this contributed heavily to his winnings. It also contributed to the making of the myth that bothers Michael Harrington so much.

In this sense, leadership has a peculiar attribute in nations we are wont to call democratic. There's always the question of who's doing the leading. Does the leader mold opinion or does he try to find out where people are and adjust accordingly? There can be no question that in recent years leadership is largely giving way to surveyed public opinion. In the film *Modern Times*, Charlie Chaplin got into trouble because he picked up a red flag that fell from a lumber truck and, while chasing the truck to return the flag, he managed to turn a corner just in front of a group of marching agitators. He was arrested as the leader, of course, which was a very good thing because many of the funniest scenes in the film were of Chaplin's jail experiences. In the more modern of modern times, leadership is not quite that accidental. We no longer wait for a group of people to march around the corner and push our man out in front. We determine by "scientific" means what people want and we package our candidate accordingly.

If this was to be a book on the reselling of the president, perhaps the book would be called "A Previously Owned President." The features of the president advertised would be his decisiveness as reflected in his new economic policy, his courage as indicated by his voyage to China, his firmness as marked by his position on welfare, his common sense in his rejection of extremism, his fairness as shown by his equal treatment of blacks and whites (unlike Democrats, who favor blacks), his devotion to traditional U.S. values as manifested by the quality of men appointed to the Supreme Court, and his sound judgment in economic matters. It might be fun to show precisely how these attributes were marketed, but such a book has been done before and I do not intend to do it again here. It is curious that in 1968 the image of "Tricky Dick" was very prominent. Four years later this picture was completely erased, and no longer was there the sneering query "Would you buy a used car from such a man?" But, instead, the question was "Would you car buyers vote for a used president?" The answer to this was a fairly resounding YES. One explanation for the switch in attitude was that the people *wanted* to see such qualities in him. The famed student of personality Henry Murray has demonstrated that hungry people, when shown ambiguous stimuli, are likely to see food. In 1972 the American people were hungry. They were ravenous in their desire to escape reality—to return to football and movie star worship—although with slight changes in sex symbols and a markedly different kind of cowboy. Richard Nixon supported and reflected such mentality.

That Nixon was seen to possess these new positive features is amply supported by evidence. A Gallup Poll (*Newsweek*, August 28, 1972) rated Nixon high in leadership qualities. The percent of the population viewing specific traits were as follows: Principled, 40%; Strong, 34%; Careful Thinking, 34%; Fair, 30%; Good in Judgment, 30%; Forward Looking, 29%; Moderate, 24%; whereas only 3% of the poll reported him to be an extremist, 12% an opportunist, and 6% old-fashioned and backward. These favorable personal attributes can be correlated with his perceived achievements while in office: 59% cited his trip to China, 54% cited his trip to Russia, 38% his Vietnam policy, 19% welfare reform, 17% law and order, 17% school busing, 15% Supreme Court appointments, and 5% dealing with dissenters.

Note how neatly his personal attributes and ascribed achievements fit into the principle of either ignoring unsolved problems or projecting a nonworkable oversimplified solution. Thus it follows that Nixon's alleged greatest achievement was obviously "peacemaker." Poverty and racism were viewed as inflated problems and Nixon was credited with stabilizing these through welfare reform, law and order, busing, dealing with dissenters (even his Supreme Court appointments) . And, because not even a credible case for environmental protection could be made, the issue was ignored. Besides, the environmentalists dirtied the political waters in many disturbing and difficult-to-understand ways, so the best way to handle this was to drive it out of political consciousness. This Bo-Peepism—America's foremost ideology—becomes a theme returned to when specific issues are created.

A part of the change in the Nixon image can be attributed

to the office itself. That's not quite as simple as it sounds. Most people once advanced to presidential status *do* become bigger than life. Suddenly discovered in some very common people are heretofore unrecognized qualities. But that doesn't always happen, and certainly the magnitude of change is different for different presidents. Some very unexciting people remain unexciting as presidents. Will Rogers did lean forward after being introduced to President Calvin Coolidge and say, "I didn't catch your name." And Dorothy Parker said, on hearing of Coolidge's death, "How can you tell?" Yet there are the others, the superheroes—the Washingtons, Jeffersons, Jacksons, Lincolns, Teddy and F. D. Roosevelt—and even worn-down and eventually totally pathetic Woodrow Wilson. It's hard to find in any of them any commonality with Richard Nixon. It certainly looked—and the polls reflected this—as if in the winter of '71 he was doomed. In more ways than it is necessary to amplify, Richard Nixon looked like L.B.J.—one sad term and then obscurity. What happened?

Get yourself into the proper perspective. Remember the duckling in his full representation of his ugliness. This Richard Nixon was the same shopworn stimulus that lost so ungraciously to John Kennedy. He was the incredible Richard Nixon who not only lost to Pat Brown, a remarkable feat in its own right as Ronald Reagan later proved, but did it so embarrassingly that all of us felt guilty even watching it. It was so bad that afterward he promised to retire and everyone was relieved, even his closest friends—much the same way most of us desire punchdrunk fighters to retire; some of us want this for the good of the game while others desire it out of compassion. But, characteristically, he didn't retire. He arose again and, with everything going for him, almost blew an election to Hubert Humphrey and with that he became president. He attained the highest, most powerful station in the world. But the ascendancy did not produce an immediate transformation of image. He continued to look like some of us believed him to be, a pathetic mismatch of ambition and talent. There was no sparkle to his administration; he did not manage to create any of the excitement of Franklin Roosevelt; his cabinet officials didn't crackle with diversity and power. He had none of the regal mannerisms of an F.D.R.; nor was he a John Kennedy who exuded romance, handsomeness, good grooming, and also a majestic presence that people want so much to see in their leader. He wasn't an Eisenhower either, an untarnished war hero with Bing Crosbyish human qualities who added to his allure with an irrepressible Charlie Wilson whose quotes added spice and a John Foster Dulles who, by playing Russian roulette with nuclear weaponry, added excitement to the administration. Nixon and all about him were dull, virtually indistinguishable from each other, and ponderous. There was no charisma anywhere.

An administration makes it in the public eye when it captures some of the magic of Camelot, a place where exciting people do things that border on the miraculous. Richard Nixon, for all of his inauspicious beginnings, did create a Camelot. Camelot, like all exciting reigns, is as much known for its supporting cast as it is for its star. Camelot had its king, an interesting (albeit faithless) queen, a magician, a superknight, a pure knight, some assorted witches, knaves, and just jolly good guys. The key man was the magician. Without Merlin there would have been no Round Table. Without Merlin the many warring kingdoms would not have been brought together for even short-term peace. And, without Merlin, the doctrine that "might is right" would never have been challenged. Merlin was not merely magician, he was also teacher and adviser; he had academic as well as sorcery credentials. Well, Richard Nixon got himself a Merlin— his name was Henry Kissinger.

Kissinger was something else. He was a true magician. In the public mind, he opened doors that defied all previous sorcerers. He conjured up a witches' brew that tamed the most obdurate foes. Kissinger gave to Nixon shades and nuances he never before had with the electorate. He gave to Nixon a virile sexuality without dirty overtones. He gave to Nixon a humor and a grace. Kissinger gave to the Nixon image what never before had been manufactured for it—*class*.

The other important Jew working for Nixon was Sammy Davis, Jr. He also added to the illusion of Camelot. Politics always has had and always should have some of the glamour of show business to capture the imagination of people. When politics becomes all show biz and no substance, however, it becomes totally corrupted. When politics no longer is a means by which power is exercised to solve problems and in which the electorate participates in meaningful ways, it degenerates into a simple charade with tragic consequences. In the United States in recent years, the distinction between entertainment and political processes has been blurred. Movie and sport stars have ascended to important positions. One of the bodies that Richard Nixon trod on in his tortuous path to the White House was movie star Helen Gahagan Douglas, wife of Melvyn Douglas. Sammy Davis, Jr., however, is not just another movie star. He, unlike John Wayne and other pro-Nixonites, hasn't always been a Republican. He, unlike Shirley MacLaine or Paul Newman, was part of the swing vote, the group that normally voted Democrat but defected in this election (and here he was joined by Frank Sinatra and his gang). He was different in many respects. He wasn't a powerful hero but, rather, he generated sympathy. He was truly an underdog. As he describes himself, "Who could be more disadvantaged than a little black Jew with one eye?" And of course there's an answer to that—lots of poor people. But, nonetheless, he generated something akin to

Galahad—the pure spirit expressing allegiance to an understanding and sympathetic liege.

Every Camelot needs its Lancelot, its superwar hero. Lancelot, in the legend, is what makes the Arthur story a tragedy. He both loves and is loved by Arthur but he betrays him in an affair with the queen—now *that* Lancelot certainly isn't a part of the Nixon legend. But there were two persons who, with a little pumping up, could take on some of the Lancelot dimensions—one is Spiro Agnew, the other is John Connally. Spiro did range the countryside in quests and jousts and, inasmuch as evidence of knighthood exploits was largely based on self-report, he emerges as a fairly plausible Lancelot. Connally, while he doesn't betray his king, does betray his party and, by doing so, he takes on the qualities of unbeatable foe. (In actual behavior, Spiro Agnew is much more like Sir Kay —loyal and inept and in his station only because the king felt sorry for him.) Connally is more like Gawain (the offspring of the witch Morgause, the queen of air and darkness), leader of the always suspect "Orkney faction," who was vile tempered, sometimes mean, once even chopped off a lady's head; but in the end lonely, brave, and loyal to Arthur, while disloyal to his surviving family.

There are others who add images of excitement. Certainly Martha Mitchell for a time played a role, and in that she was not too far removed from Morgan Le Fay (another witch, sister to Arthur and Morgause), particularly as she is described so unkindly by T. H. White in her strange castle, guarded by griffins, secret service men, FBI, and other supernaturals—stretched out on "a bed of glorious lard"* and the only thing missing was a telephone.

Every legend with a hero must also have a villain. In the Arthur legend, the villain was Mordred, the back-stabbing, mother-killing hunchback, illegitimate son and heir apparent

* T. H. White, *The Once and Future and King* (New York: Putnam, 1966), p. 111.

to the king. It was his plotting that finally brought the vision down. With Nixon there can be conjured up a succession of Mordreds. One, indeed, for each of his crises—from Alger Hiss to Walter Bickel to Charles Goodell (although Spiro Agnew called *him* "the Christine Jorgensen of politics") to George McGovern himself.

The Arthur legend is a tragedy. It's a tragedy of a king who tried desperately to forge a "new majority," who won over dissidents of the opposing party (the Orkney faction; interestingly enough, the Irish), who tried even to generate a new morality in the quest for the Holy Grail but in the end was alone, beaten, betrayed by the few he loved—and all this happened, perhaps (although T. H. White doesn't carry it that far), because he had no real visions—no solutions to poverty, to racism, or to war. His closest friend was a warrior, not a thinker, and there may be in *that* more King Arthur in Richard Nixon than any of us want.

Legends really generate from only two aspects of leadership that have been discussed up to now—the projected images of the ruler and the felt needs of the people. Legends are likely to persist when these two dimensions are at odds with the ruler's real qualities and the real but not understood requirements of the people. Arthur is a legend that kept a vision of a united kingdom alive for centuries when it was torn from within and without. Other legends fulfill the same need. Solomon, the last of the great Israelite kings, is wise in legend; but, in truth, wisdom certainly wasn't among Solomon's qualities. His profligate tax schemes and his efforts to create a majestic Jerusalem (he was not so ambitious to want yet others in San Clemente or on the coast of Florida) brought a shaky alliance of tribes to an end. The ensuing bickering among them left them disunited and easy prey for powerful foes. But the legend of Solomon and a reunited Israel persisted and became a driving force for that nation's re-creation. Thus myths and legends are forces for political mobilization but rarely lead to political resolution. The Orkney faction returns in the IRA. The problems surrounding Israel won't evaporate with mere exhortation.

When the other dimensions of leadership are considered, the authentic attributes of the leader in relation to actual problems and the possible available alternatives to solution, the regal picture of castles and round tables dissolves and in its place we find Oz—with Nixon as the wizard enlarging himself by means of primitive television; Kissinger as the Straw Man looking for a brain; Laird as the Tin Woodsman; Agnew as the Cowardly Lion; and each of us as Dorothy— and when we awake we will realize that we have been hit by something like a cyclone and things are in a very bad way in Kansas and elsewhere.

The inner Richard Nixon is of little relevance to this book. Whether he is stable and profound or shaky emotionally and intellectually is important only in the context of his public leadership demonstrated in the key issues dealt with here—peace, employment, social equality, social justice, and environmental protection. If one wants to find the real Nixon, go elsewhere, and there are lots of places to go because Nixonologists are everywhere. Bela Kornitzer, Ralph De Toledano, Earl Mazo, and Steven Hess have written favorably about the president; the president has lauded himself autobiographically in his *Six Crises.* But not so kind things have been said about him by Bruce Mazlisch in a book entitled *In Search of Nixon: A Psychohistorical Inquiry* and by Garry Wills in *Nixon Agonistes: The Crisis of a Self-Made Man.* Probably the most exhaustive and possibly the most devastating book has been written by a British journalist, Arthur Woodstone, entitled *Nixon's Head* and published in May 1972.*

It is the purpose of this book, however, to examine the

* Olympia Press, London.

public aspects of Nixon's leadership and his correspondence to democratic ideals. Nixon emerged from his first term with a virtually unscathed public reputation. It is my intention to prove that he acted dictatorially and was inept, and yet neither the undermining of democratic institutions nor his failures at achievement were brought to light. And if these charges are true, how can I reconcile them with the previous statement crediting the American voter with intelligence? There's no contradiction here. The American voter does the best he can with the knowledge at his disposal. The reelection of Richard Nixon was no reflection on the electorate's intelligence; it was, however, a manifestation of voter ignorance.

Legends are created in the absence of solid education. A gap in our education is in the area of understanding leadership in the democratic context. This plays an extremely important part in the Nixon story. In every conceivable sense, Nixon as president has had a free ride. The opposition party gave him no trouble. Congress, with a constitutional mandate to provide a check and a balance on the president, capitulated to him. No models for leadership worthy of emulation emerged outside of the electoral process. Schools contributed to the degeneration of the democratic process by offering nothing which could possibly assist students to evaluate leadership.

There were five Democrats in position to exercise leadership during Nixon's first term: Edmund Muskie, Hubert Humphrey, Ted Kennedy, George McGovern, and William Fulbright. Each in his own way failed. Muskie just refused to act. As natural leader and odds-on favorite to become the party's standard-bearer at the next election, he attempted to placate a torn party by not taking a stand. Coyness for short periods is difficult to take, but a three-year's sustained marathon of it is nauseating. As chief centralist of the Democratic party, Muskie is living proof of the indefensibility of the underlying logic of the Committee for a Democratic Majority —he tried to unite by disregarding contradictions. A huge military budget is not reconcilable with social legislation; an unguided, growing economy is not reconcilable with a livable earth; an organized labor retrogressive stance is unalterably opposed to minority rights. When the party you lead chooses to tear itself apart by running off in different directions, as leader you have choices. You can try to risk all by bringing it back as a coordinated body through presentation of an integrated position or you can pretend the divisions aren't there and keep quiet. Muskie chose discretion—it's reputed to be a Maine trait—and the party stagnated.

Hubert Humphrey isn't from Maine, which is regrettable because in him silence would have been a virtue. He was silent for a time after 1968, licking wounds as a college professor, but he returned to the political wars as a Minnesota senator in 1970. And, when all other challenges fell by the wayside, he belatedly decided to seek the Democratic nomination for president and in that effort to try to stop McGovern from being named on the first ballot. There's obviously nothing wrong with that—in fact, a spirited primary campaign is healthy—but the means that Humphrey used were Nixonish. In California, the last important primary, Humphrey in opportunistic desperation threw away all principle in his attacks on McGovern. Humphrey's personal diatribes became the heart of the Democrats for Nixon arguments against McGovern.

McGovern, who went after and won the primary, also failed to play a significant role as party leader in the Senate prior to his ascendancy to the candidacy. He, too, was jockeying for position while Nixon was consolidating his leadership. McGovern never articulated a clear alternative to the president's leadership.

Ted Kennedy's failures are obviously the most easy to understand. He was, for a variety of excellent reasons, reluctant to seize the reins of the party. But his presence, given the current state of public consciousness, reflected leadership, and he too must bear some responsibility for not coming forth with a contrasting comprehensive plan for America's future.

Fulbright, as chairman of the Senate Committee on Foreign Relations, had a leadership role that he never pushed through. In the absence of the old tigers, Wayne Morse in particular, the outrageous excursions and war-provoking behavior of the administration gained almost a sense of respectability because of Fulbright's refined bearing. He too chose not to stomp the nation-sounding alarm, and he too was unable to offer a new course of action for the United States in the realm of international behavior.

Congress as a whole surrendered its sovereignty to the president. Congress does have certain powers, among them control of the purse strings. And Congress, as Wayne Morse so persuasively has argued, failed even to educate the American people about constitutional authority. When the president refuses to spend money Congress appropriates, this impounding is unconstitutional (especially when Congress overrides a veto), and yet the president gets away with it. No credit to him, but even greater discredit to a body whose job it is to provide the boundaries within which the president can function. Because Congress as a whole capitulates, it's relatively easy to discount the few members who stand up and fulfill their responsibilities. It is up to us now to give to those who try to make the system work, to give to congressional dissidents the greatest opportunity to be heard; to generate in the next few years forums and debates of excitement and substance.

Outside of electoral politics, leadership based on violence (at least of rhetoric if not of behavior) was rapidly losing favor. Bayard Rustin, one of the moderate blacks in the formation of a Committee for a Democratic Majority, hit home when he analyzed what happened to Black Power (*Newsweek*, November 13, 1972).

> We hear little from those who popularized Black Power and in turn became household names to the notoriety it generated. Stokely Carmichael lives in Africa—he has dismissed America as unreconstructably racist and from time to time issues statements of praise for one of Africa's most brutal dictators. H. Rap Brown is in jail. Eldridge Cleaver is in exile under house arrest in Algeria, a nation we are told is the vanguard of the Third World revolution. Floyd McKissick, a super militant of CORE days, is today a real estate entrepreneur and a militant Republican.

There are some weaknesses here. Rustin seems to have ignored other militants who fared better—Huey Newton and Bobby Seale who survived and even broadened a base in Oakland, California; the success of radicals in elections in Berkeley, California; and the emerging of a United Raza movement with vigorous importance in the Southwest.

His argument does have considerable strength, however, when he recognizes and is willing to accept a considerable amount of the responsibility.

> Much of the blame for this situation must be shared by those of us blacks, who through ignorance or cowardice, refused to challenge Black Power and its spokesmen. Our white allies—liberals, students and church leaders—also bear responsibility.

Then he makes a statement that seems to me completely indefensible.

> Only organized labor continued to press for those reforms that served all of society's exploited and thus could bring about the basic changes impossible to realize in marches and demonstrations.

Here is where I feel the arguments of Rustin and those like

him fall completely apart. Where is the labor leadership? Who would we turn to? Certainly not George Meany; and, if not George Meany, who else? And, without any identifiable leader, who makes their presence known to the rest of us? Rustin is wise enough to recognize that organized labor cannot do it all alone; he understands the need for new allies; he talks much as we have here about the need to generate "a broad-based coalition which embraces intellectuals, organized labor, young people, minorities and liberals." But he leaves out the leadership function; where is there an identifiable person to lead such a coalition? Perhaps in the very last analysis, because he is unwilling to look to the importance of leadership, Rustin makes, I believe, a very serious logical error—he confuses cause and effect. He argues:

> Perhaps the most destructive influence on that coalition has been Black Power and the new tribalism it engendered.

That's not it. Black Power and the new tribalism emerged as a *result* of the vacuum of leadership among white liberals; it was a reflection of confusion, of aimlessness, of guilt without political purpose. Needed now are clearly defined, logically congruent political causes and someone with courage and access to the microphone to take the helm. Only if that kind of leadership emerges in the labor movement can the labor movement again claim to be a force for reform.

If the schools would truly function to educate people for the role of being citizens in a democratic society, included in the school program would be a variety of activities, experiences, and knowledge exchange now missing. There would be a much more extended discussion on the importance and true understanding of individual rights, the workings of our government, and, perhaps most important, there would be discussion about the attributes of leadership within the context of democracy. Currently, schools indoctrinate; they refuse to educate. True education would involve a serious analysis of our society and all of its problems and would systematically discuss democracy as an unrealized ideal with the citizen engaging in constant vigil over those whom it allows to serve in elevated elected positions. The student in school would discuss such matters as natural progression to higher offices —there is currently no logical way to become president, there is no sequence of responsibility. Students would be constructing criteria for evaluating leadership capabilities and learning to distinguish democratic from authoritarian leaders.

I would postulate at least five ways in which a democratic leader differs from a dictator, and they are the following:

1. *Leader accountability.* Democratic leaders defend decisions with logic and evidence. They go before any challenger, particularly the most severe critics, to ensure a market place for idea exchange. Dictators would either refuse to discuss matters or in extreme cases would attack the questioner.

2. *Leader negotiability.* Democratic leaders sit down and try to ameliorate differences in a society. They realize that wisdom is not owned by one individual or faction, and that give-and-take is part of the democratic process. Dictators do not negotiate; they dismiss negotiation as manifestation of personal weaknesses.

3. *Leader as recognizer of irreconcilable differences.* Democratic leaders appreciate that some differences based on principle cannot be reconciled. The key is that they respect the rights of those who choose different paths and encourage the opposition to present its case before the people. Dictators don't recognize the legitimacy of differences. To dictators, differences are almost synonymous with treason.

4. *Leader appreciation of differences.* Democratic leaders appreciate diversity among their nations, religions, ethnic groups, races, classes, and political ideologies. They recognize that the entire nation benefits from its heterogeneity. Dictators impose single norms and standards and insist there is only one right way to do things.

5. *Leadership in relationship to rules and society's ends.* Democratic leaders recognize the relationship of rules to ends. They are aware of the need of flexibility and understand that law and order is meaningful only in the context of justice. Dictators do not allow the questioning of law; they apply it with a heavy hand and favor certain, severe punishment for law violators.*

The absence of loyal opposition, alternative leader models, or education is a condition favoring greater authoritarian rule. If, for example, one accepts as tests of democratic leadership the guides outlined above, it is clear that Richard Nixon flunked all of them.

- He steadfastly refuses to be accountable to anyone and most particularly to his critics.
- He even refused to debate his principal opponent in a presidential election.
- He refuses to negotiate even with dissidents within his own party, and even when he changes in direction in policy, he does it without apparent consultation.
- He rejects diversity; he wants everyone to be alike. He doesn't understand that difference in style and temperament may represent differences in social identity.
- He pretends to accept irreconcilable differences but, in the absence of debate, this becomes not only meaningless, but a means by which ideas can be dismissed.
- He is a law-and-order man without considering justice or mitigating circumstances.

These failures become increasingly apparent in the way key issues are treated—Richard Nixon's deficiencies as leader of a free people are reflected in his "crusade for peace." A matter which is taken up next.

* For a more extended discussion of education for democracy, see Arthur Pearl, *The Atrocity of Education* (New York: Dutton, 1972).

CHAPTER FIVE

War is peace
OR,
How the Grinch stole Christmas

Richard Nixon got reelected, at least in part, because of his image as peacemaker. According to Daniel Yankelovich's polls, that was the key factor in his reelection. During the campaign an unwavering 62 percent of the voters said, "Mr. Nixon is doing everything he can to end the war" (*New York Review of Books*, March 30, 1972). But, again, image and reality bear little relationship to each other. In reality, Richard Nixon engaged in more irresponsible brinksmanship and outright war action than any other president in our history. He authorized the invasion of two countries (Laos and Cambodia), he mined an international harbor (Haiphong), and he stepped up the bombing, which resulted in the destruction of friendly embassies and deaths among our allies. None of these acts was endorsed in advance by Congress and none, ironically, gained any military, economic, or political advantage except for Richard Milhous Nixon.

When the greatest warmonger in our history gets reelected with one of the largest pluralities ever because he is seen as "Mr. Peace," then you do have some mighty fine fooling going on.

Let's review the acts of aggression again and analyze how Richard Nixon was able to turn them to his advantage. Prior to April 30, 1970, and the Cambodia incursion, Richard Nixon had offered little inkling of his preelection proclamation of a secret plan to end the war in Vietnam. In June 1969, after a meeting with General Thieu, he announced the beginning of troop withdrawals. On November 3, 1969, he unveiled "Vietnamization," a plan whereby the war would continue with U.S. dollars and aircraft but with Vietnamese ground troops. If King George III had hit on such a plan during our Revolutionary War, he would have called it "Hessianization." In that speech, Nixon made his appeal to the "Silent Majority," who in time would become the mainstay of his "New Majority." The American he successfully wooed was not much interested in politics, distrusted eggheads, and loved his country in the same way deserting fathers love their children. The speech was intended to cut off the growing peace movement which, according to polls, was beginning to draw into it the blue-collar workers, businessmen, middle-income housewives, and so on. That peace movement planned and carried off the greatest gathering for peace ever held in the United States on November 15 when crowds estimated at half a million paraded before the White House. This was the high point of the peace movement. Too bad Mr. Nixon missed it—he was out of town in Florida attending to other important things.

Periodically, Nixon continued to disclose new troop withdrawals. Less than two weeks before the Cambodian invasion, he went before the American people to report that 150,000 more boys would be brought home from Vietnam before May 1971. His announcement of troop withdrawals was having its effect on peace forces, which were running out of steam. But his acts of aggression did them in. On April 30, after the incursion had begun, Nixon let it be known that he had authorized a military invasion of a neutral country—Cambodia—because

> North Vietnam had not respected Cambodian neutrality . . . the enemy was stepping up guerrilla activities and building up to launch massive attacks. . . . Cambodia, as a result of this, has sent a call to the U.S.

All of this evil had been perpetrated by the enemy, according to Nixon, after we had done so much for peace. "Let's look at the record," said Mr. Nixon, "we have stopped the bombing of North Vietnam, we have announced a withdrawal of over 250,000 of our men. The answer of our enemy has been intransigence at the conference table, belligerence at Hanoi, massive military aggression in Laos and Cambodia and stepped-up attacks in South Vietnam designed to increase American casualties."

Looking at the record is always a desirable activity, and we too should look at it from a variety of perspectives. First, let's give every dubious point to Mr. Nixon: that indeed Cambodia called for help, that the Vietnamese had established definable, easy-to-wipe-out sanctuaries for hit-and-run military activities, and that American casualties would increase because of this unfair North Vietnamese advantage. Conceding all this, the invasion of Cambodia was still an irresponsible and outrageous act. An invasion of a country, regardless of justification, is an act of war and the United States Congress, not the president, declares war. Congress wasn't even informed in advance. Members of the Senate Committee on Foreign Relations complained that they learned about the invasion when everybody else did—when the president told them about it on television and radio.

When one examines the record at all closely, however, it is

no longer possible to concede either assumptions or matters of fact to the president. It is extremely doubtful if Cambodia's General Lon Nol ever called for help. It is certainly dubious that anything could be accomplished militarily by such a venture. It is even dubious if General Lon Nol was a legitimate head of state since he seized control in a military coup when Prince Sihanouk was out of the country, and there was no indication then or now that he has any popular support. There are other facts in the record undermining the president's credibility. At first, he argued that only South Vietnamese would be used as ground troops to clean out "Parrot's Beak" and "Fishbook," but later it was disclosed that U.S. personnel did indeed take part in the ground action.

By his actions in Cambodia, Nixon demonstrated the dictatorial attributes ascribed to him in the last chapter. He refused to be accountable, to go before elected officials and present a plan and defend it with logic and evidence. Presenting the matter as a *fait accompli*, he precluded any possibility of negotiations. While allowing that some persons disagreed with him, he never credited that disagreement with open debate. He continued a war of attrition on *The New York Times* and the *Washington Post* for their audacity in disagreeing with him. He tolerated no diversity of opinion within his own shop. Walter Hickel had to go. And there was, in the Cambodian invasion, absolutely no connection of means and ends.

The Cambodian adventure was meaningless from any standpoint. It gained nothing. The war went on and in fact the military situation continued to deteriorate, prompting later actions, for example, the mining of Haiphong. The invasion of Cambodia was a blunder and it should have finished Richard Nixon; in fact, in a typical orgy of lugubrious self-pity, he predicted "that the move against enemy sanctuaries will make me a one-term president" (April 30, 1970). To the contrary, Cambodia and other similar acts led to his resounding victory.

Nixon did not stop with Cambodia. On January 30, 1971, he invaded Laos. The justification here was to cut off enemy supply lines. But neither Cambodia nor Laos were big deals. It didn't take too much courage for the world's most powerful nation to take on countries one-tenth its size with one-hundredth of its technical sophistication. He still had a biggie left. In the spring of 1972, he ordered the mining of Haiphong harbor, an act which in effect threatened all the big powers, including China which he had recently visited and Russia which he was about to visit. This was a declaration of war—United States against all comers. He got away with each of these acts. This in itself is surprising, but even stranger was the fact that each in an odd way added to his image as peacemaker. That a series of warlike actions should enhance a peace image needs explaining. A multiplicity of factors led to this seemingly unlikely occurrence.

Among the reasons that Nixon was so able to transform his belligerency into apparent serenity were: (1) he generated a new set of rules; (2) he exploited the weaknesses of the peace advocates; (3) he continuously inspired hope that "peace is on hand"; and (4) he gained curious support from the Chinese and Russians. Each of these conditions requires some specification. Very quickly in his regime, Nixon made the number of ground troops in Vietnam the single criterion on which war or peace was to be based. He established a scoring system easy to understand and giving the impression of rapid and continual progress. Thus he was able to create an illusion of peace while he increased the geographic areas of hostilities and markedly stepped up his air war. More bombs were dropped on an almost defenseless North Vietnam in the Nixon regime than had ever been dropped before and in fact the intensity of bombing was greater in the *winding-down* phase of the war than any other similar activity in history. The costs of the war and of war preparation remained high. Nixon was particularly coy in budget analyses. He would ask for one figure in his budget address and then send Secretary of Defense Laird to Congress with requests for supplementary funds. The latter funds were always included as part of a big victory or a severe threat and made to appear as bargains, as offers one couldn't refuse. In 1972 Nixon asked Congress for the second largest military budget in U.S. history—an increase over the previous years—and still had the audacity to claim that it represented a cut in defense spending.* In his defense budget, Nixon got help from the dream killers at the Brookings Institute, for example, where a counterbudget with scaled-down military expenses was calculated; this budget was in the same ball park as the president's and it gave the impression that the differences debated were relatively small and concerned sophisticated matters beyond the understanding of ordinary folk.

In his scoring system, Nixon exploited the limited education of the U.S. citizenry. He knew they had almost no experience with large numbers. He realized that their knowledge of geography was limited, but that they did know boys in Vietnam—they had friends, neighbors, or relatives there—reduce that number and by that feat alone create an illusion that the war would soon be over.

Regardless of any evidence to the contrary, every Nixon

---

* As comparison, the total military budget in the Johnson administration (4 years in which he served as elected chief executive) was $257 billion, or an average of $64.25 billion per year, whereas Nixon's military budget in his first term was $317.20 billion, or an average of $79.3 billion. (Source: *Statistical Abstract* [Washington, D.C., Bureau of Census, Government Printing Office]). Both underrate the actual expenditures and Nixon's disguise of war spending is more extreme than Johnson's. But, any way you calculate, it's no way to wind down a war.

action was heralded as successful. Thus Cambodia and Laos were trumpeted as effective deterrents of enemy aggressiveness and mining of Haiphong as the act that drove the North Vietnamese to serious negotiations. Once he was reelected, the war erupted again in an escalated form. The notion that Nixon's behavior was in the interests of peace continued to have some credibility. The *London Daily Telegraph* synopsized this outlook:

> Mr. Nixon is acting on the assumption that it was the earlier bombing of the North and mining of Haiphong, coupled with the defeat of the Communists' spring and summer invasion that brought them back to serious negotiations and it will do so again. He may well be right. He is exercising power in a just cause.

All of this was not particularly new—in fact it was very old. Here we find a psychological phenomenon known as *déjà vu*, the feeling that somehow or other we have been here before. Since the beginning, we claimed nonexistent victories in Vietnam. Since the beginning, General Westmoreland developed the war's philosophy—the more it doesn't work, the more we have to do it, and we can't quit now with victory just around the corner. This was the stuff that did in Lyndon Johnson. How come it paid off so handsomely for Nixon? Well, he added a new dimension in the mining of Haiphong. He reinjected pride in the war. No longer were we the bully getting whipped by a little kid half our size, we were now picking on someone our own size. Nixon injected some drama in what had become the dreariest of all wars. This could be it—that heart-stopping, tingling, thrilling, and potentially horrifying moment in history. The Haiphong mining came at a time when the war was going badly (when hadn't that been?) with confidence in Nixon (according to the Harris Poll) slipping fast and McGovern, campaigning for the primaries, capturing the peace mood of the country.

Then boom, it all changed. The dull, drab Nixon had captured some of the allure of John F. Kennedy.

According to Daniel Yankelovich's polls, Haiphong produced the following psychological effects:

> The days that followed reminded voters of the Cuban Missile Crisis. People were anxious: "How would the Russians react?" "Would they cancel the Summit?" "Would they try to break the blockade by force?" even "Would there be a nuclear confrontation?" When the Russians announced that the Summit would go on as planned, the public, as our surveys later showed, was vastly relieved. With mounting confidence, they watched the drama unfold on television: Mr. Nixon being greeted coolly but correctly at the Moscow airport; meeting in a somewhat more cordial atmosphere with Brezhnev; being toasted at Soviet banquets; addressing the Russian people; laying a wreath at the grave of a little Russian girl orphaned by the war; signing documents and treaties of historic importance with the head of the Soviet state.
>
> Slowly, almost imperceptibly, the message got through to the American public: Nixon had faced the Russians down, and the danger to the U.S. from the war—the danger of a big power confrontation—had been defused. The war in Vietnam would now soon be over. Or, even if it did not end right away, it would no longer be seen as a military threat to Americans. Soviet/Chinese acquiescence in the Haiphong mining had handed Mr. Nixon an overwhelming diplomatic victory, containing the seeds of his subsequent political victory at home. Vietnam, we found, is the issue of greatest concern to the American public, and in the public mind it was almost as if the war had ended at the Moscow Summit (*New York Review of Books*, November 30, 1972).

Haiphong did establish for Nixon an initiative and, once ahead, he stayed ahead—but the seeds of his victory began two years before in Cambodia with the shattering of the peace movement. The strong peace voices were gone. The two giants who stood up, Wayne Morse and Ernest Gruening, were defeated in elections that brought Nixon to power. No longer did the Senate Committee on Foreign Relations push the administration to be accountable—no longer was it possible for Wayne Morse to hold what he called "seminars" (his critics called them "filibusters") on the Senate floor. The *Washington Post* and *The New York Times*, the major newspapers critical of Nixon's behavior, were being subjected to head-on continuous attacks by Spiro Agnew and intermittent oblique assaults by the president himself. But neither the lack of powerful peace voices in the legislature nor those in the media were the significant factors in Nixon's free ride to the White House. Nixon gained a peace image when the peace movement shattered into a series of convulsions after the invasion of Cambodia.

For years there have been many different groups trying to develop a public consciousness for peace. All have been small and only minimally effective. But peace in Vietnam became a significantly large movement. It started small and on campuses in "teach-ins" which exposed first students and then others to the fact of our involvement in South East Asia. It ended where it started—on campus!

After the Cambodian invasion, the campuses erupted. University communities, horrified by the president's arbitrary action and driven to desperate frustration, responded with one empty symbolic act after another. But the one theme that umbrellaed all of the reaction was "strike." Universities, nationwide, went on strike in response to the Cambodian invasion. Strike in a university means that classes aren't held, that students do other things instead. In the strike after the Cambodian invasion, some students sat in at the university presidents' offices—others marched to the city halls—others to the ROTC buildings or to the draft induction centers —others played cards—some few, very few, set fire to buildings—some students tried to engage persons with different views in serious debates—some circulated petitions in support of Hatfield-McGovern's proposal for a date certain when all of our troops would be removed from Vietnam—others worked for peace candidates running for office—some taunted policemen and national guardsmen—others just stood around to watch the excitement. Almost every campus had some excitement, some violence, some destruction, some tear gas, some mace. But Kent State and Jackson State had the most.

On May 4, 1970, on the campus of Kent State University in Ohio, national guardsmen, in·one of the many such confrontations, killed four students and wounded several others. A few days later, in Jackson State University in Mississippi, a similar occurrence took place and somehow, with these two acts, the issue of war disappeared and suddenly the number one problem facing the United States was "student unrest." The growing alliance of workers, businessmen, housewives, and students for peace was ruptured, never to be reknit again during the first term of the Nixon administration. That Nixon was able to turn things around to his advantage was a neat trick, but it was unplanned. He did not invade Cambodia to provoke the students into behavior unacceptable to a broader population. This was pure luck: Nixon was one of the three Princes of Serendip, who botch up everything they touch but in the process make unanticipated discoveries. As later events proved, Nixon invaded Cambodia because his basic beliefs about war never changed. In public, he expressed the opinion that peace at home and abroad was won by decisive show of force. Apart from a few "agents provocateurs" (undercover FBI agents and hired informants),* who have played minor roles in campus uprisings, the campus response was out of Nixon's control, reflecting the inadequacies of the peace movement.

* See Frank Donner's *The Confessions of an FBI Informer* (New York: Harper and Row, 1972) for a fascinating case study of how the agent provokes violence.

Even the term "strike," as a nationwide university reverber-
ation to Cambodia, was unfortunate—the term irritated the
blue-collar worker in particular. The students were making a
mockery of something that wasn't theirs to play with. *Strikes*
are economic weapons through which employers are damaged
or embarrassed through a systematic withdrawal of labor.
Obviously, a student "strike" could do neither. A strike to a
blue-collar worker is a serious matter; he gives up something
precious—his wages. The term strike irked the unionist; he
saw the students going off on vacations which he, the unionist, paid for with his taxes. Here the students were very similar
to Nixon in their lack of accountability. They didn't get sanc-
tions for such behavior from organized labor. To the contrary, they became the "bums" that Agnew incessantly and
Nixon frequently referred to as images of opposition to their
programs. The college students became collectively Archie
Bunker's sons-in-law; "know-it-all freeloaders—not dry
behind their ears telling their betters what to do." Cambodia
marked the end of any unified campus activity. The rupture
had been coming for a long time, probably since the Democratic convention of 1968 when the radical on campus, by
rhetoric and style, was losing support among any range of students—radical politics just wasn't fun and students as a whole
didn't like violence and senseless destruction. They
responded by trying to ignore the issues, and fewer and fewer
people showed up at "free speech" platforms. Football, drugs,
religions of all sorts and orthodoxies, right-wing politics, and
return to traditional study replaced political action and even
the responsible political efforts to respond to Cambodia were
sad: the groundwork for such actions wasn't laid; the petitions didn't have a sustaining force behind them. The peace
candidates (and in 1970 there were many running for
national and state office) saw their campaign and campaigners swept away in the aftermath of Cambodia and Kent State.
I speak here out of personal experience. I was running in

the primary election to be the Democratic candidate for governor of Oregon. The campaign had aroused considerable interest, but of the 11 candidates running for governor—8 Democrats and 3 Republicans—I alone spoke out against senseless violence. As I put it, I was the only candidate against illegal violence at home and abroad. My condemnation of student irresponsibility led to a university newspaper editorial "Art Pearl Shows His True Colors" attacking me for my opposition to their violence and for taking issue with them that anything could be accomplished by something called a "strike." But my biggest problem was with the outside community—everywhere, in factories, supermarkets, and taverns, as if to find some release for pent-up emotions, the campus became the deflection that people seek when either the problems at hand won't go away or the solution is being disrupted, and "student unrest" was a very soluble problem. If the war wouldn't go away, no matter what anyone would do, there were more solutions available for campus problems than there were restless students: there could be arrests, suspensions, expulsions, tax cutbacks, and investigations.

One anecdote might capture the temper of the times. I was campaigning in the eastern part of Oregon about ten days before the primary election on May 25, 1970, ten days after Kent State. I was in a small tavern inhabited mostly by native Americans, a group of people with a set of real, unresolved grievances against every branch of government. My volunteer staff introduced me to the crowd and I spoke a very few minutes and asked if there were questions—there was ONE. One person in the crowd demanded to know where I stood on student unrest!

All that has been presented up to now is Old Nixon, involving the kinds of things he had done before—inventing rules and scoring systems, claiming big victories in exaggerated crises and taking advantage of a discredited opposition, and they were part of his losing tradition. There was still a missing component, something to complement his total lack of subtlety. Haiphong, which had given him some pazzazz, would not likely have been sustained and could indeed have backfired. He needed some other illusions that the war was drawing to a close. Here's where Merlin the Magician reenters. Henry Kissinger was able to exploit a vital psychological phenomenon—hope. Hope does spring eternal. People's wants are desperately transformed into beliefs. Psychological experiments have demonstrated this over and over again. Stotland, in his book *Psychology of Hope*, emphasizes that hope requires a belief in the credibility of the event happening. Kissinger made peace credible. He provided a seemingly unassailable set of arguments and achievements. After a series of meetings in far-off magical places, almost again Camelotish in nature, as if questing for the Holy Grail, Kissinger had done it. He had managed the impossible. He got everybody to agree—the Russians, the Chinese, the North Vietnamese, the South Vietnamese—to a plan and he was able to announce on October 26, 1972, just two weeks before the election, that "peace is at hand." And that's how the grinch did it. He stole our annual Christmas wish, peace on earth, and, unlike Dr. Seuss's children's story, we never got it back.

"Peace is at hand," my foot. Two months later, after the reelection of Nixon, the war broke out in renewed, unprecedented fury. The people had been fooled again, not because of any intellectual deficiency but because of educational deficiency. There is a ceasefire in Vietnam but there will be no peace—peace is much more than just an end to open hostility. Nixon might be sincere in his efforts to achieve peace, but he is never real. It is important here to reduce Kissinger to his actual dimensions. Richard Nixon didn't happen on Henry Kissinger like Arthur was fated to stumble onto

Merlin; Kissinger got his position because he too believed in the deterrence effects of military strength and manifested a willingness to use such power. Kissinger, as I. F. Stone has pointed out, is a veteran cold warrior; he attained his prominence through Pentagon patronage. His first published book, *Nuclear Weapons and Foreign Policy*, reflected the depth of his allegiance to Pentagon mentality. He was for years adviser and consultant to the Rockefeller brothers. (In 1968, when still working for Rockefeller, he expressed horror at the prospect of Richard Nixon for president.) Even as far back as 1958, he warned about Communist takeovers in places like Greece and Indo-China. He was among an orbit of intellectuals who argued for peace through balanced terror and diversified weaponry. Whatever illusion and allusion Kissinger has of his resemblance to Metternich, alleged stabilizer of post-Napoleonic Europe (about whom he wrote sympathetically), the truth is that Kissinger played no stabilizing role in the Nixon administration. He merely did what he was told. But he had a confident style and he was believable. I. F. Stone put Kissinger down to size and described his true role in the Nixon administration:

> Kissinger has conned his way to the top in Washington; he is a master of seductive arts. Amid the dull plastic men at the White House he shines out by his self-disparaging humor (in this he is Jewish rather than German), by his wit, and by his sophistication. He says what Nixon says, but with a smoothness and subtlety that stirs admiration. He is willing to listen to opposing points of view with an understanding often deceptive; the understanding look is often taken for agreement. He can, without compromising himself, create the most contradictory impressions, depending on whom he happens to be talking to and wishes to impress. The newspapermen—and despite the hard-boiled stereotype we are all pretty naïve and pushovers for a bit of charm—call him "Henry" affectionately. A little of his performance may even rub off on his master.

He is a skillful actor. With peaceniks he makes himself
out a bit of a martyr, a hurt and misunderstood little
Jewish boy. He not only makes you feel he understands
your concerns; he is good at telling you what *your* concerns
are. He asks what you would do in his place—a skillful way
of creating a bond between him and his interlocutor.

With those on the other side he is the hard-boiled master
of *realpolitik* who will not sacrifice one iota of American
interest. Thus while he tells one side that the North Vietnamese could have what they want if they would only trust
him and be patient and stop being such pernickety "little
lawyers"—as he recently put it to Norman Mailer—he tells
journalists on the right that he is working to maintain
American power in Vietnam (*New York Review of Books*,
November 2, 1972).

Kissinger is true "vision killer." His "muscular liberalism,"
a term ascribed to him in David Landau's semicritical biogra-
phy *Kissinger: The Uses of Power*, emphasizes the muscles
and distorts any concept of liberality. Basically, Kissinger
doesn't trust people. He wants decisions to be made at the
top by firm men; his liberalism always deals with power—
never with justice. His liberalism requires controlling of the
basic evil of man's nature with external forces. He never for a
moment entertains a vision that men could rise to higher stations without arsenals and ordnance depots. Kissinger doesn't
dream of peace, he dreams of tactics and strategy for make-
shift agreements, negotiated balancing of terror—as if somehow we can attain sanity if I keep *Psycho* locked in my cellar
while you keep the Boston Strangler locked in yours.

Kissinger may represent a slight change in Nixon philosophy, although this is never clear and certainly not consistent.
Kissinger may have prevailed upon Nixon to renounce military victory in favor of some stable balance in Vietnam which
would come about through developed understanding of those
who have the power—the United States, the USSR, and
China. The entente of the United States, Russia, and China,

Richard J. Whalen says in his book *Catch a Falling Flag*, was *the* essence of Nixon's secret peace plan. This is hardly peace but, rather, a perpetual updating of unending uneasy cold war with small powers sacrificed as pawns to large-power interest—that game is subject to change as powers grow or decline. (Remember that just a few years ago the "major" powers in the world, at least by official definition, were the United States, Russia, France, England, and Taiwan.)

In January 1969, Kissinger, in the magazine *Foreign Affairs*, outlined his plan for resolving the Vietnam dilemma. He rejected then an outright military victory. He was critical of either a coalition government or a ceasefire. He sought, instead, some sort of staged U.S. military withdrawal with a corresponding beefing up of South Vietnamese military authority as the basis of "honorable" U.S. disengagement from Vietnam. Thus, at the very beginning of the administration, one can detect the taking shape of "Vietnamization" and "troop withdrawals," which were to become the catchwords of the Nixon administration.

When, in mid-December 1972, it looked as if a ceasefire and a military disengagement were "at hand," Anthony Lewis commented on the success of Kissinger's 1969 announced plan. He conceded that Kissinger had succeeded in separating "the two tracks, the military and the political" —and he reflected on the costs of four years of Kissingering around.

> He did not tell us that he would have to drop another 4 million tons of bombs on Indochina to achieve our negotiating objectives in part. Or spend another 20,000 American lives. Or send another 50,000 soldiers home with serious wounds.
>
> Nor did Kissinger have, or convey, any idea of what it would cost the people of the two Vietnams, Laos and Cambodia to have his minimum negotiating aims reached. He did not tell us that South Vietnam alone would suffer

upwards of 80,000 soldiers killed and 240,000 wounded, 16,5000 civilians dead and 400,000 wounded, an estimated 1.85 million made homeless.

It is fair to say that Kissinger probably did not envisage costs of that kind when he published his negotiating formula. For he wrote that he did not believe a "prolonged" negotiation was possible. What, then, went wrong, so far as we can identify it, on the American side of the talks?—the Nixon administration attempted for years to do the inconsistent things. It tried to settle with Hanoi by persuading it that the political future in the South would be open. At the same time it was helping to build Thieu into a figure with enormous military and autocratic political power.

After these four years South Vietnam has 1 million men under arms—the equivalent of 12 million in the United States in terms of population. Thieu's police force numbers 119,000; 15,000 or 20,000 of those in the special branch. Thousands of civilians are held in prison without trial, among them some of the independent non-Communists with whom Americans would naturally identify (*International Herald Tribune*, December 13, 1972).

On December 18, when the war was renewed with the heaviest air attacks ever and with the increased costs—in dollars, in human suffering, in American prisoners of war—all illusions about Kissinger should have gone with it, but by then the elections were over and the renewal of hostilities wasn't universally applauded. The *London Daily Mirror* editorialized:

To Richard Milhous Nixon, that frustrated, glib and secretive man in the White House, this may make sense as a tactic designed to bring the Communists back to the negotiating table. To everyone else it is an act of insane ferocity. A crude exercise in the politics of terror. A blunder of tragic magnitude. It will serve only to blacken Richard Nixon's name—in the color of dried blood (quoted in *Rome Daily American*, December 13, 1972).

And the always hawkish *U.S. News and World Report* (Jan-

89

uary 1, 1973) explained why the war dragged and why the negotiations failed. The North Vietnamese and the Viet Cong refused to concede that the land they occupied and won at such terrible costs really belonged "to the Saigon government." Inasmuch as that's what they were fighting about, it is hardly likely that they could concede such a vital point; thus it was unlikely that on such a basis peace would ever be at hand. All the negotiations were senseless exercises.

One needed no negotiations or a Kissinger with his Metternich complexes to get out of Vietnam. We had got there and stayed there on the basis of lies (as the *Pentagon Papers* amply demonstrated). We maintained a succession of fabrications for our presence, including the arguments leading to the resumption of hostilities. We went to save democracy when it is clear (and even General Ky, the former vice president of South Vietnam, later agreed) that General Thieu's reign was, as Diem's was before him, a reign of terror and suppression. We went because we were bound by treaty—only we found ourselves without allies. We went to prevent a bloodbath, and later bragged about our kill ratios. We went to protect our troops, although who would attack them if they were to leave since this would be what the "enemy" wanted? And, finally, we stayed to recover our prisoners of war. The obvious was really never given the consideration it deserved.

Through fear and overstatement and senseless noise and provocative distortions with Viet Cong flags and insignias, the pristine simple solution to our Vietnam involvement never got into the market place: we could, at any time, have left as we entered, unilaterally and without negotiation. We could have gotten out with no more dishonor than renewal of the bombing or a subsequently negotiated ceasefire has brought us, with no more bloodbaths than we ourselves have produced and no less democracy than General Thieu represents.

We could have left any time during the past four years and our POWs would have followed shortly. I say this authoritatively, without ever sitting in on a high-level conference or being privy to a secret document; I say it out of some knowledge of human behavior. The "enemy" Vietnamese behavior is logical and consistent: they wanted the United States out of Vietnam. They wanted *all* Americans out, including POWs. The POWs were a bargaining instrument, about the only one they had. Once we left, there would be no need to keep them. And one thing is certain: even Nixon (and those militarists around him) would allow that the North Vietnamese and the Viet Cong are not stupid; they know that if the POWs were *not* returned, the United States *would return,* the bombing would resume, the destruction would be intensified. Once the United States got out of Vietnam, the POWs would follow shortly and no Kissinger was needed to work out the details of this.

And now to the Chinese and Russian role in the creation of the Nixon image. Nixon's trip to China was voted by the AP editors and news directors as the number one news story of 1972 (December 27). Daniel Yankelovich, in his argument on why Nixon won the election (*New York Review of Books,* November 30, 1972), concluded that

> Mr. Nixon can thank the Soviet Union for handing him his most important political victory. The Russians virtually pushed Mr. Nixon back into the White House when they agreed to go ahead with the Summit meeting after the mining of Haiphong.

The general impression given by Yankelovich and also by I. F. Stone in a series of articles in the *New York Review of Books* is that Nixon pulled off a big coup—Stone bitterly denounces China and Russia for assisting Nixon in his psychological warfare against the North Vietnamese. Stone is correct but somewhat naïve: he discovered anew what had become general knowledge—Russia always takes care of Russia first (and now apparently the same thing can be said of China). China's and Russia's national interests far outweigh any international ideological commitments—the discovery of this prompted Arthur Koestler to write *Darkness at Noon* and he, André Gide, Richard Wright, and Ignazio Silone to state their disillusionment with communism in the book *The God That Failed*. What hasn't been analyzed is Russia's and China's willingness and perhaps even desire to have Nixon in the White House.

Nixon enhanced his image by going to Russia and China —of that there can be no question—but he also elevated the prestige and honor of those in power in Russia and China (who, in the vagaries of their systems, are constantly standing for reelection). In both China and Russia the hosts determined the nature of the visits; they enlarged their images and fabricated their own Camelots with *their* people.

Both China and Russia have much to gain from the United States—the reverse might not be true. Both nations are in need of vital resources and technological development, and this they may have gained from the Nixon visits. Meanwhile, these visits didn't appear to lessen Russian military support to North Vietnam and, in fact, the Russians' post-Nixon visit offerings may have been an improvement in both quantity and quality considering the success antiaircraft barrages had on our bombers after the hostilities were renewed.

It well might be that the Chinese and Russians desire a continued American military presence in Southeast Asia. For the Russians, the Vietnamese war provides a proving ground, an opportunity to test our weaponry without human casualties—for example, there were never any Russian POWs in South Vietnam clamoring to be returned. The Russians and Chinese are able to keep the costs of our military involvement up at only a fraction of their own; our presence in Southeast Asia serves the propaganda purposes of both China and Russia and justifies military incursions of their own. The U.S. Army at the Chinese border provides a psychological pull for national unity and deflects attention away from unresolved problems at home. A warring United States in Southeast Asia also keeps the USSR and China from any escalation of *their* serious disputes. And, finally, for both parties the longer the war dragged on, the more it sapped the morale and reserves of the U.S. people and the less likely that the American people would respond to a real threat. That Russia and China refused to respond recklessly to the gauntlets thrown at them does not mean that they won't when such a response is perceived to serve their interests. Again, it would seem that the most likely explanation for Russia's and China's behavior is that they are getting what they want from U.S. policy.

It might also be that the Chinese and Russians like Nixon as president. From their perspective, *they* faced *him* down and got him to leave Vietnam on their terms. They may be content with his domestic policies, seeing in them corruption, selfishness, and dehumanization that will leave the American people unable to match communist competition in any domain.

Wouldn't it be strange if, despite all his history of anticommunism—his role in the Alger Hiss case, his irresponsible attacks on Helen Gahagan Douglas, his kitchen debates with Khrushchev—Richard Nixon the super anticommunist, by his visits to China and Russia, ends up as the Manchurian Candidate, the man who unwittingly serves the interests of worldwide communism at the expense of freedom and peace at home?

The image of Nixon, peacemaker, and other warmongers like him will remain distorted until a true peace movement emerges in the United States. Even if Russia and China or any other power wanted to play less self-serving roles, they could do little to help us. The responsibility for a peaceful America rests solely with the American people. Therein lies the vital missing component: the absence of a force for peace. There are religious pronouncements. On December 22, 1972, the top church leaders of the United States denounced the president for his resumption of bombing in exceedingly strong language, "betraying the duty of peace," "vindictive barbarity," and "irresponsible assault" (AP, December 22, 1972). On the same day a pathetically small group of perhaps one thousand marched in protest in New York City, prompting Tom Higgins, president of the National Student Movement, to observe that "protest is not in season ... it's a combination of semester break, final exams and Christmas" (AP, December 22, 1972). Therein lies the problem—periodic marches and episodic pronouncements do not a peace movement make. Until we understand why we failed to generate a peace movement in response to the longest and most unpopular war in our history, the Richard Nixons and all others like him will continue, almost like Zodiac killers, pleading to be stopped before they kill again—and there will be no one to stop them.

The peace movement, when it was growing, never really qualified as a true movement—it was a loose aggregation of persons wanting the war to end. It never had visions of what peace on earth really means. It never had organization for staying power. It never was a movement for "all seasons." It was vague, general, sectarian, and basically, apolitical—and, ultimately, peace is a political problem—encompassing four different elements of political action: public education, elections, lobbying, and, in support of the other three activities, rare confrontations (boycotts or protest marches).

There was no organizational sense to the movement. It

94

developed no large dues-paying membership, no periodical for mass enlightenment; it never immersed itself in electoral politics and evaluation or selection of candidates and it never established ideological limits.

On campus, the movement degenerated in time to gonadal rather than cerebral need gratification—particularly in its slogans and confrontations with police and the national guard. Many students were in the movement to their ankles only. They were not for peace in any general sense, they just personally didn't want to fight, and when Richard Nixon reduced the importance of the draft he reduced the student concern about war appreciably. If the students lost interest in peace for narrow, selfish reasons, organized labor maintained interest in war for equally selfish reasons: they were made to believe that, if peace broke out, unemployment would surely rise and those working in defense industries had particular cause to worry. This fear was never dealt with and furthered the estrangement between the student and the factory worker. Even minority youth were pulled to support the war —unable to gain psychological fulfillment anywhere else, the military offered them belonging, usefulness, competence, and a curious form of security—and, again, this kind of conflict at a basic level was left unattended by the peace movement.

The lack of any formal organization produced a problem in the development of leadership. People emerged as instant leaders and disappeared almost as quickly. In situations like this, demagoguery has a lot going for it; the wilder the claim, the more likely one may be credited as leader—at least, by a hostile press and a television hungering for scenes of burning buildings and bludgeoned bodies. Thus, in time, the peace movement was captured by violence, property destruction, grotesque theatre, and empty rhetoric. There was no substance or sustenance—no persistent pressure. Even more true and less defensible was Bayard Rustin's complaint about

Black Power—to paraphrase him, much of the blame for the situation must be shared by those of us concerned about peace who, through ignorance or cowardice, refused to challenge the spokesman for peace through violence.

Other problems impeded the development of a true peace movement. One was a strange hybrid bird, half dove (the Far East side), half hawk (the Near East portion). Nixon gained considerably because of this confusion and because the situation was never clarified and because no proposals for a total peace were developed: long-term pacifists became transformed into the "new realists," the vision killers who justified wars by reasoning thusly: What else can little Israel do? Would you have her be devoured by her enemies which surround her?

Peace is a particular problem for the Democratic party, which has, since 1946, been the war party. It was the Truman Doctrine that proclaimed the United States role as world policeman, this policy giving military aid to French and Dutch efforts to regain their Asian colonies, which they had forsaken to the Japanese in World War II. It was under Democratic party regimes that the war escalated, and cold warriors and hot warriors tore the party apart during the 1972 primaries. The issue of war or peace is one the Committee for a Democratic Majority would like to avoid or compromise. But there is no avoiding or compromising such an issue. As a nation, we either go it alone and participate in or watch little wars until one day all hell breaks loose, or we develop a solid basis for peace keeping through multilateral authority by restoring, reforming, and enhancing the United Nations. Multilateral peace keeping is as much a part of Democratic party tradition as is warmaking; Woodrow Wilson first proposed a League of Nations and Franklin Delano Roosevelt, a United Nations Organization.

Liberal dream killers will argue that the United Nations

has no power, and of course they are right. The United Nations cannot have power if the most powerful nation in the world subverts it and generates treaties outside of it, such as NATO and SEATO, and if it engages in wars, then of course it mutilates the United Nations. A unilateral withdrawal from Vietnam, recommended here, would not produce peace any more than would a negotiated pact, but it would make it possible for a multilateral body to act, not only in Vietnam, but also in Ireland, Egypt, and anywhere else that war should happen to erupt. The failure to maintain a continued debate on how this can best be done was yet another serious deficiency among peace advocates during the sixties.

A true peace movement deals with fundamental issues. That peace movement can emerge learning from the flaws of the past decade. Peace is a costly proposition and, once the guns have been muzzled, the bombers grounded and "our boys" home with their loved ones, the American people may not be prepared to pay the price of peace. They may be dazzled anew by Nixon and his Merlin—the dynamic duo who plucked victory from the jaws of disaster—and forget, if they ever knew, that nothing was accomplished in 1973 that could not have been gained on October 26, 1972—or, for that matter, January 26, 1969. In point of unassailable fact, the agreements reached in the winter of 1973 offered more to the "enemy" than was ceded in the Geneva accords of 1954, which the United States refused to sign. In 1954 the North Vietnamese (then known as the Vietminh) *agreed* to return to the North. In 1973 the United States *agreed* to let the North Vietnamese remain in the South which, according to President Nixon, is very "honorable."

If activities for and thoughts about peace are allowed to decline after U.S. *overt* military involvement in Vietnam has stopped, the consequences can be nothing less than tragic.

The immediate threat of war continues in the Far East, but also in the Near East, Latin America, Africa, everywhere. The lack of a significant peace presence places ultimate and complete power in the hands of a president who has distinguished himself only by unilateral, precipitous, and unpredictable behavior. In a period of less than three months, he flip-flopped from peace to war to peace again. This kind of leadership needs the eternal vigilance of a powerful peace movement.

The threats to peace will not evaporate if we close our eyes to them. The state of a mass self-inflicted blindness is what led us into Vietnam in the first place. An effective peace movement is, more than anything else, a help-the-blind movement. The end to hostilities in Vietnam offers both an impedance and a promise for true peace. The chief barrier is the distinct possibility that, because of our direct military disengagement, the American people will be lulled back into an almost comatose state.

The desire to forget a miserable and disgraceful episode of United States history is certainly understandable from a psychological perspective. Human beings will strive for emotional equilibrium by driving from their minds unhappy or intolerable thoughts. Freudian-oriented psychologists call this "defensive mechanism repression." Undoubtedly, there will be a widespread tendency to repress all the unpleasantness associated with Vietnam and to generalize such feelings to all peace activities. Such impulses certainly undermined public support of peace activities after World Wars I and II when peace advocates, finding themselves almost alone, muttered something like "I can't believe they forgot the whole thing." This forgetting will doubtless take place if past miseries are emphasized. A peace movement does not need to fall by the wayside if future advantages are stressed. The end to hostilities provides opportunities as well as problems for peace advocates. The peace movement can be disencumbered from some distractions. When not actively at war, it is more difficult to slander the peacemakers as abetting enemies and at such times the advocates of peace do not have to shout over jeering jingoists to be heard. They just have difficulty getting anyone to listen.

Peace will be won only if the dynamics of human decision making are fully appreciated and understood. On every truly important issue, humans go through a phenomenological cost-benefit analysis; this means that, from a unique and personal perspective, the "pros" of a decision are weighed against the "cons." A true peace movement will stress the positive attributes of true peace and relate such a potential to quality of life concerns. Such a peace program must transcend platitudes of "brotherhood" and really, as my black friends say, "get down." In concrete and specific terms, peace must be related to quality of life—security, comfort, belonging, competence, and usefulness in every arena of life—work, politics, culture, aesthetics, leisure, and interpersonal relations.

A true peace movement must also communicate the "cons" of war thinking as well as warmaking and cost these out in day-to-day experiences. The public must also be alerted to the expense of peace—the need to relinquish some nationalism and the uncertainty that accompanies such action. It must also be made to know that a true peace may require significant changes in life style particularly in the expenditure of earth's resources on trinketry. But, in this context, a public must be made aware that in refusing to reach for a true peace they might have to surrender their lives. Some fundamental issues need attention for a world at peace; these include the distribution of wealth, racial relationships, historical enmities, and ecological matters.

A true peace would require new nonexploitive relations

between the "have" and "have not" nations: true equal opportunity and social justice for nonwhites, conciliation and mandatory arbitration of historical disputes, and a fair share of earth's finite resources for all its peoples.

In all of the above the United States is in a position of leadership which it cannot relinquish. Our presence affects every human on earth. We dominate the world economically, we have the most sophisticated technology, we are the greatest squanderer of the earth's depletable resources, we own the greatest military might, and the tentacles of our economic activity are found everywhere. We have the potential to lead the world to a just and lasting peace. We need a movement to do just that.

A rejuvenated peace movement would have the following components: (1) a plan for marked reduction in U.S. military spending; (2) a commitment to strengthened multilateral peace keeping through a beefed-up United Nations; (3) a refusal to side with any belligerent state; (4) a rejection of violence, thrashing, or other infantilisms as tactics; (5) the recognition of the political responsibility of a peace movement; (6) an obligation to offer plans for reduction of underlying drives toward war; (7) a forum for drawing into the market place of serious debate worldwide analyses and specific proposals for reduction of tensions.

Now for a few caveats. The movement cannot be too broad; it cannot be so common that it loses sight of its cause. It would exclude those unwilling to address underlying causes of wars. Thus it would be more than a gathering for prayer and recitation of liturgy. It would exclude those wanting peace while maintaining the economic and social status quo, thus excluding those who would restrict the movement to only a few elite purists. It would also exclude those prohibiting debate, those too timid to offer proposals, and those so audacious as to believe that only *their* plan is valid.

Such a movement could draw into it the labor leaders that Bayard Rustin (*Newsweek*) and Michael Harrington (*The Nation*) and the Committee for a Democratic Majority all want somehow to be a part of America's political future. The recruitment must be selective. Only labor leaders who want peace, who are able to generate visions of full employment without dependency on the defense industry, would be invited. It would draw into it businessmen aware that our present course is suicidal. It would draw into it minorities, women, and youth. It would be the common major force for reshaping our destiny.

Peace movements don't spring up spontaneously. That's one lesson that surely was learned from the sixties. Planning is vital and first steps are critical. A true peace movement could perhaps begin as follows: One hundred distinguished persons, broadly represented, committed to peace, could come together. They would include every segment of the United States. They could come in response to a call from Wayne Morse and Ernest Gruening (whose solitary votes against the Gulf of Tonkin resolution gave them special status), although others with equally impeccable peace credentials could serve as well. This committee of 100 would bring $100 each and pledge $10 a month more, thus establishing sufficient funds for a national office. They would also resolve to recruit at least 10 others within a month. Each of these, in turn, would make commitments similar to those of the original 100. Therefore, the initial invitations would be extended only to persons with established constituencies, although special exceptions would be made for persons representing the poverty-stricken. Thus, within a month after its inauguration, the national peace movement would have a capital investment of $100,000 and a monthly income of $10,000. This group would develop a three-focus thrust for peace:

1. It would be involved in public education through a monthly publication called *Peace*. This periodical would provide an analysis in depth from multiple perspectives and would be modeled somewhat on the format of *Fortune* magazine. For example, one issue could be devoted to the Near East in which the official position of the Arab states and of Israel would be represented and three neutral experts would respond with individual assessments and proposals for a lasting peace. It would be the aim of such a publication to gain within a year a subscription list of 5 million people and almost that many more periodic readers from newsstand sales.

2. The initial group would be used to establish a mass dues-paying membership with regional, state, and local organizations to meet regularly, discuss issues, keep in touch with elected officials, organize forums, and hold seminars. Chapters could be organized on campus and in every union group, in religious organizations and in neighborhoods. The target membership at the end of one year would be in excess of one million dues-paying members. Dues paying would be established on an ability to pay, but income expected from dues would be approximately $1 million a month. Chapters could be organized by members of the original organizing group of 1,000 traveling to campus, engaging in group discussions, debating issues with persons still supporting military and bellicose activities, providing membership cards, and following up on regional and state bases to ensure that the groups sustain themselves and that, if local leaders default in their responsibilities, others willing to take on and fulfill these responsibilities take their place.

3. The new peace movement would become intimately involved in electoral politics. Annually, the magazine *Peace* would rate all legislators on their peace activities, providing opportunity for rebuttal and debate, selecting 100 critical house and senate seats for election of peace candidates in 1974.

The schools must become involved with peace education. Today children go to school to learn about war, mostly indirectly through history lessons in which they are taught that we never lost a war or won a massacre. Students are never given knotty problems to solve; they never understand the logic underlying the United Nations or the consequences of other alternatives. They are never given the responsibility for designing and defending a model program for peace. At the university level, the commitment to peace education should be even more intense. As a prerequisite for graduation, regardless of major, every student should be required to offer a plan for world peace and then to defend that plan in terms of his discipline or major area of interest. In developing adequate education for peace, *Peace* magazine could provide teachers with curriculum materials. Debates could be arranged by the peace organization with any persons who are proponents of war or other military intervention; but, in addition to that, special programs should be offered for training and retraining teachers.

At the present time, only the University of Hawaii and Michigan State have peace education programs for prospective teachers. By 1975 there should be at least five centers training teachers to help elementary and secondary school children learn about the intricacies of international relationships and the futility of violent solutions to national disagreements. If the federal government cannot be prevailed upon to provide funds for these institutions, private foundations ought to be approached. If all else fails, the development of such centers would become a responsibility of the peace movement.

The mass media, at the present time, attempt to exalt and even wallow in violence; motion pictures, and television tend to describe enemies as subhuman and allies as superhuman. The new realism in both films and television tends to make all of us into mindless amoral brutes. *Thoreau* would make as good a movie as *Patton*. Heroines in the long history of women concerned for peace would make as exciting a movie as heroines of the roller derby. Leo Szilard or Albert Einstein are as worthy of depiction as Billy the Kid or Butch Cassidy. Again, the peace movement would try to persuade mass media to engage in activities that would promote peace. Failing, the movement would take upon itself responsibility for development of such media.

In summary, voters were fooled into believing that Richard Nixon stood for peace. Richard Nixon shares some blame for this, but the major responsibility lies with the weaknesses of peace advocates. The business of creating a valid peace movement must have top priority or else we are likely to be fooled again, and one of these days we will have reached a point of no return.

CHAPTER SIX

Any able-bodied man can
  OR,
With all that unemployment there
must be jobs somewhere

There once was a prizefighter named Al "Bummy" Davis. Bummy Davis was not well liked; on the contrary, he was hated because he didn't fight clean—he hit low, gouged eyes, rabbit-punched, and did other things like that. Once he fought Fritzie Zivic, an equally hard-nosed guy from Pittsburgh, and in their fight it was reported that not one fair blow was struck by either party. Lots of people would come to watch Bummy Davis fight. They came to cheer his opponent and Bummy's introduction was always followed by a thundering chorus of "boos," whereupon he would turn, face the audience, grab the ropes, and shout, "That's okay, suckers —you paid." Bummy Davis died a hero. He was shot trying to stop the robbery of a candy store.

Bummy Davis and Richard Nixon might have much in common: neither was known to fight fair, both could end up heroes, and both operate on the philosophy "Okay, suckers—you paid."

One of the most expensive aspects of American life during the past four years, second only to conduct of the war, was the president's performance in matters concerning work. In any way expense is calculated—economically in dollars, psychologically in human gratification, environmentally in destruction of earth's resources, morally in sense of national purpose —the American people paid handsomely for the dubious privilege of the Nixon presidency and very likely will pay even more during his second term. The basic thesis presented here is that in foreign affairs Mr. Nixon got away with murder—while at home he got away with highway robbery.

The reason for his domestic success parallels, but is not identical with, the development of his image as peacemaker. He profited from an almost universal ignorance about economics—from a total lack of intellectual leadership from any quarter, the decline of "traditional" "liberal" labor, and proliferation of myths which tended to add congestion to an already messy situation. The president's response to any complicated matter is stereotypic—he simplifies it! It is immaterial that the simplification destroys any resemblance to reality. In politics *reality* is defined by votes. And if the president generates something that *he* appears to understand and it sounds somewhat convincing to a constituent "new majority," *that* becomes reality. The logic is clear—the Richard Nixon success is predicated on an extension of the notion that in a nation of blind men the one-eyed man is king and, ergo, in a nation of the totally blind, the *president* must also be without vision.

As with the war, Richard Nixon relied heavily on his scoring system. With the war, progress was measured in "troop withdrawals." With "work," progress was measured in "official unemployment" and "official rates of inflation." The former index indicated the activity which enabled people to work, while the latter was interpreted as a measure of value received for the work. On both variables the president claimed unprecedented success—later, the claims of reduction in unemployment and inflation will be examined. But first it is imperative to understand the legitimacy of voter confusion on domestic issues.

Work as a presidential responsibility is far more muddled in the public's mind than is the office's responsibility for peace keeping. There is substantial agreement that the president is a factor (some believe too much so) in the declaration of war, but there is no such consensus that his office or any other governmental agency has an obligation to "declare work." President Nixon is but one of a considerable number who advocate that government remain aloof from such a mundane matter. The core of his position is summarized in one phrase of his second inaugural address: "Ask not what your government can do for you, ask what you can do for yourself" (January 20, 1973). In that simple sentence Richard Nixon's essence is revealed. He is the Hollywood that Oscar Levant analyzed when he said that once you get under its superficial exterior tinsel you get down to its real tinsel. In that one pompous platitude, Richard Nixon justifies his malfeasance, misfeasance, and nonfeasance of office and in that wretched nonsensical statement is reflected the total intellectual anarchy omnipresent in his discussions of work.

Confusion cuts deeply into every aspect of work. There exist no well-defined suggestions for determining the optimum *number* of jobs for the United States or the world. How much of that work *should* be manufactured goods and how much *should* be human service? How *should* work be divided: by age, race, or sex? How *should* people be prepared for work? What measures, if any, *should* be used to evaluate work potential? What *should* be done for the unemployed,

107

underemployed, handicapped, and adults not in the labor force? How *should* work be made more rewarding for *both* the worker and the clients and customers served by the work? Richard Nixon has offered very little leadership in any of these areas. He is not alone. Alleged experts haven't helped either by focusing on only one aspect of a problem or by talking past each other. In this chapter, an outline of a comprehensive plan for work is advanced and placed in contrast with the situation we find ourselves in. But, first, an assessment of the Nixon era and its impact on the economic life of our society. It must be remembered that Mr. Nixon, more than other recent Republican candidates, drew support from ordinary working people. I submit they were badly fooled and that Mr. Nixon, while not perfectly clear but nonetheless unmistakable, used his office to create havoc in the work world. More so than any post–World War II president, Richard Nixon acted to

- increase the ranks of the unemployed (unemployment "rates" increased by a full percent during the first four years of Nixon's rule and unemployed persons increased by over 60 percent; no other president since the depression days had so dismal a record).
- divert work activities away from ecologically defensible activities such as education, health, welfare, esthetics, recreation, and conservation.
- stop the decline in sex and race inequality in work activities (at the end of his first term, while he claimed to have used his influence to reduce unemployment in general, unemployment for nonwhites remained twice as high as for whites; unemployment rates for men decreased whereas women's unemployment rose).
- assist the wealthy to be even wealthier (by a variety of governmental actions—direct subsidies, tax loopholes, and governmental contracts—monies were given the rich

and the super rich at the expense of potential job creation of unemployed and others who were not allowed entry into the labor force).

• ignore the decline in worker satisfaction by using his office as a coercive influence to force workers back into unpleasant activities (this he did primarily through vetoing the development of new jobs and by establishing "workfare" for the indigent).

• undermine the credibility of public service employment by disparaging remarks, by appointment of political hacks to high executive positions, and by brutalization by "efficiency" experts (in education, health, welfare, and poverty programs, human concerns were bypassed in favor of bureaucratic intransigence and inappropriate accounting schemes; the president, by his own remoteness from the people he ostensibly served, set an example of arrogant indifference which has come to characterize Nixon's administrative style from top to bottom).

These are fairly harsh accusations. It is now time to establish whether they have any validity.

First, let's look at unemployment in Nixonland

It may profit readers to review briefly the Nixon record on unemployment and contrast it with the other post–World War II presidents. First, a caveat, even something seemingly as simple as unemployment, isn't that simple. A person must be in the labor force actively searching for work to be classified as unemployed. Take 1971 as an example. On an average day in 1971, 5.0 million people were classified as *unemployed* and 79.1 million people were on someone's payroll—that calculates out to a total labor force of 84.1 million, or a 6.0 percent unemployment rate. There were others around in a kind

109

of limbo, however, according to the official *Manpower Report of the President*.* They were neither working nor unemployed. They were not in the labor force. In 1971 those over the age of 16 not in the labor force averaged out to 55.7 million people. That's a lot of folk, folks. It's more than ten times as large as the "official" unemployment and over two-thirds the number of those working.

The large number of "Not in Labor Force" adds an interesting dimension to unemployment statistics. If the sole criteria for *good* employment is reduction of "official" *rates* of unemployment, there are three ways to go: (1) create new jobs; (2) encourage people out of the labor force; or (3) *claim* the creation of new jobs. Mr. Nixon chose the last. How this occurred is best understood against the backdrop of an official press release on the last month of the first term of Richard Nixon. This is what Mr. and Ms. Citizen read in early January 1973:†

> The total number of Americans at work rose 280,000 to 82.8 million last month, while the nation's unemployment rate remained unchanged at 5.2 per cent of the work force, the government said today.
>
> The number of jobless Americans actually edged down 150,000 to 4.1 million, but this is expected in December and the Labor Department figured it as no change on a seasonally adjusted basis.
>
> The report, rounding up employment developments over the past year, noted that the unemployment total was down 600,000 in the past 12 months.
>
> The report by the Bureau of Labor Statistics also said that average earnings of some 50 million rank-and-file workers rose $1.12 to $139.50 per week in December and were up $8.20 or 6.2 per cent over the past year.
>
> Workers lost 3.5 per cent of their purchasing power to rising living costs over the year, leaving them with a net gain in pay of 2.7 per cent.

* Washington, D.C.: U.S. Department of Labor, 1972.
† *Santa Cruz* (California) *Sentinel*, January 5, 1973.

The report said that the nation's total employment rose over the year by 2.4 million.

"The nation's employment situation during 1972 was highlighted by strong labor force and employment gains and a moderate decline in unemployment," the report said.

It said the average employment total of 82.6 million in the final quarter of the year was an all-time high and was 3.6 million above mid-1971.

The December total of 82.8 million also was an all-time high.

In December, the unemployment rate for men edged down from 3.6 per cent to 3.4 per cent with a total of 1.7 million.

The jobless rate for women edged up from 5 per cent to 5.1 per cent with a total of 1.3 million. The rate for teenagers rose from 15.4 per cent to 16 per cent with a total of 1.1 million.

President Nixon's chief economic advisor, Herbert Stein, said the 5.2 per cent jobless rate achieved the administration's goal of reducing unemployment to "the neighborhood of 5 per cent" by year end.

"1972 has been a year of substantial progress in reducing unemployment," Stein said in a statement, recalling that the jobless rate was 6 per cent a year earlier.

He said the rise in December employment was "particularly encouraging" and that further gains could be expected in 1973.

Now who can fault that—more people working than ever before, with unemployment down 600,000—although it wasn't so good for women or youth or minorities. Unemployment for blacks was at 9.2 percent, twice the average of whites and unchanged in 1972 from the record of 1971.

But do not cavil. Let's look at the accomplishments. How about that all-time high in employment? Isn't that something? It sure is. It isn't quite a lie—and it isn't exactly the truth. Undeniably, more people worked in 1972 than worked in 1772 or 1872 or any year in between—that, however, is only half the story; what is left out is another undeniable fact: more people *were not working in 1972* than were ever *not working* in any other year in our history!

The Nixon administration, in comparison to other recent administrations, does not fare as well as its ad men would have you believe. When one looks at adults not working (unemployed and those not in the labor force), more than 60 million were not working at the end of his first term. This constituted an increase of over 5 million in just four years; as the following table shows, no other president was able to do as much harm in so short a time.

TABLE 1
Comparisons of post–World War II presidents' records on adults not working (unemployed and not in labor force)

President	Beginning	End	Net gain
Truman, 2nd	44.7	45.0	.3
Eisenhower, 1st	45.0	47.1	2.1
Eisenhower, 2nd	47.1	51.5	4.4
Kennedy-Johnson	51.5	55.2	3.7
Johnson	55.2	56.1	.9
Nixon, 1st	56.1	61.3	5.2

After one look at the real record of Richard Nixon, even Lyndon Johnson begins to look good and only Eisenhower's second term (and Nixon's second term as vice president) is anywhere near as bad. In fact, when one compares the average record of Republican and Democratic administrations on that one dimension, the difference is unmistakably in favor of the Democrats.

TABLE 2
Gain in nonworking populations since World War II

Democratic administrations	1.6 million per year
Republican administrations	3.6 million per year

Some might argue that it isn't fair to muddy the waters with persons not in the labor force—the old, the young, the women, and the handicapped—and it is true that some people are not in the position to work but that's hardly 56 million people. In fact, according to the president's own official report, the sole reason 4.4 million people were out of the labor force was because they couldn't find a job. That 4.4 million should at the very least be added to the unemployed, making a total of 9.4 million unemployed and raising the rate to 10.6 percent!*

Richard Nixon doesn't fare too well when examined according to his own scoring system. Even here, his record is miserable when compared to other post–World War II presidents. Under Nixon, unemployment reached a post–World War II high of 5.0 million and 1.7 million more people were out of work at the end of his first term than at the beginning, thereby reversing a steady decline in official unemployment rates over the previous eight years.

Come on now, be fair. Aren't you going to give him credit for his last year's accomplishment—that drop of over a half million unemployed? you ask.

By a strange coincidence, unemployment always seems to drop during presidential election years. The 1972 gain should be taken as an indication of what a president could do if he was on the job for all four years, but even the 1972 record is suspect—at the year's end, the unemployed was 4.1 million and that was almost 50 percent more than the average unemployment of the last year of the Johnson administration. The only thing that can be said is that Richard Nixon in 1972 compared to Richard Nixon in 1971 looks good. But then no one looks bad when compared to Richard Nixon.

Unemployment cannot be judged out of temporal context. The key to unemployment is obviously trends. Past employment has an effect on the present and the future. Perhaps the

* *Manpower*

best indication of Nixon's impact on the labor force is the growth in employment each year he was in office. During the Kennedy-Johnson years average employment jumped more than 2 percent per year. During Richard Nixon's first term the average spurt was 1.5 percent per year. The employment growth flattened out when Richard Nixon took office and, while the 1972 figures are impressive, they lose some of that allure when 1971, a year of almost no job growth, is considered. If Richard Nixon had maintained the 2 percent growth per year of employment that was the record of his predecessors, the number of people working in 1972 would have increased by well over a million.

The loss of potential work is a pretty steep price to pay for the more than one million not working, for their families, and for the rest of us, deprived of possible contributions to our quality of life—"That's okay, suckers—*you* paid."

The examination of unemployment in the United States brings to light a prominent characteristic of the Nixon administration—the misuse of statistics. Disraeli once commented that there are three kinds of lies: lies, damn lies, and statistics. Richard Nixon added a fourth dimension—he and his staff didn't lie with figures, they chose very carefully the statistics they shared with the public. They used rates and percentages when they weren't appropriate. They chose *not* to talk about the ever-growing numbers of adults who are not in the labor force. They made comparisons invalid from any perspective, rather like the M.D. who wanted credit because his dying patient was in better shape than people in a nearby cemetery. They soft-pedaled the work problems of minorities, youth, and women, thus implementing Daniel Patrick Moynihan's proposal of "benign neglect." They even assured themselves of the kind of reporting they wanted by transferring key personnel from the Bureau of Labor Statistics. But, mostly, they relied on the ignorance and gullibility of the public. All that paid off handsomely.

Hold it, don't get carried away again, get back to the point: Why blame Nixon for all that unemployment? What responsibility does he have for such a problem?

Presidential behavior influences all work. A president *directly* influences work through activities involving the determination of the federal budget. He and his staff prepare the budget for Congress to consider, if Congress appropriates funds he has the constitutional power to veto the legislation, and further extending beyond his constitutional authority he impounds (refuses to spend) money that Congress appropriates. (Richard Nixon wasn't the first president to impound funds, but he has been by far more arrogant and excessive in this distortion of power than all other presidents.) In every instance, Richard Nixon has thrown his support behind capital-intensive ventures (such as the military) rather than labor-intensive work (such as education, health, welfare, recreation, or conservation). He proposes increases in the military which go more and more for hardware (bombs, bombers, missiles, electronic equipment, etc.) and *vetoes* or *impounds* educational and environmental appropriations which would create work. In recent years he vetoed a child care bill of $5 billion because he said such an act was inflationary and would sovietize our children (it wouldn't do either of those horrible things) ; such a bill, however, would create hundreds of thousands of work opportunities primarily for women (whose unemployment rates were rising at year end 1972). More recently, he has promised to impound funds appropriated for pollution control, again on the spurious grounds that such expenditures are inflationary.

By his actions in work, President Nixon has managed to (1) increase unemployment, (2) curtail needed human services, and (3) threaten the livability of our environment. When it comes to work, Richard Nixon, like so many football players he obviously admires, is a genuine triple threat.

The situation for women and nonwhites demonstrates the rubbery nature of Nixon's statistics. He claimed to have helped both populations. In his introduction to the *Manpower Report of the President* (March 1972), he claimed that he had introduced special programs to help the minorities through

> the expansion of enrollment in federally assisted manpower programs to record figures, providing a substantial increase for Negroes and other minorities.

In the body of the report, the president and the staff of the secretary of labor claim to have made giant steps toward achieving equal employment opportunity.

> The Federal Government has recently taken the lead in reducing the special handicaps that women encounter in the labor market (p. 22).

It is evident that the president didn't see fit to overcome the special handicaps of minorities and women in his cabinet or Supreme Court appointments, something presidents before him were able to do, demonstrating once again that his practice had little to do with his preaching.

But his claims were again inflated. As the following table indicates, the gap between white and nonwhite income, after the impact of inflation was adjusted, rose steadily during the early sixties. The passage of the Johnson social legislation began to narrow the gap, particularly in the flush of its first couple of years, but by 1968 in the morass of political division surrounding Vietnam, the Great Society floundered. Income differences increased and "benign neglect" left the favored position of whites virtually unchanged.

116

Significantly, when income is adjusted for inflation, *both* whites and nonwhites lost money during the first years of Richard Nixon's first term. For whites the decline was from $10,822 in 1969 to $10,672 in 1971 or a loss of $150 income for median families. For nonwhites the drop was from $6,847 in 1969 to $6,714 in 1971 or a loss of $133 per median family.

Never during the Kennedy-Johnson terms did either whites or nonwhites lose median income from one year to the next.

Losing money is one healthy indication of what a presidency costs, and on that indicator Mr. Nixon cost both whites and nonwhites, and that in our classification system is just about everybody.

TABLE 3

Differences in median family income by race of family head—white vs. nonwhite

1960–1971 (in 1971 dollars)

Year	White income	Negro and other races	Difference in income
1960	7,982	4,416	3,566
1961	8,109	4,321	3,788
1962	8,353	4,456	3,897
1963	8,664	4,596	4,068
1964	8,956	5,012	3,944
1965	9,311	5,160	4,151
1966	9,729	5,824	3,905
1967	10,014	6,234	3,780
1968	10,404	6,508	3,896
1969	10,822	6,847	3,975
1970	10,674	6,809	3,865
1971	10,672	6,714	3,958

SOURCE: *Current Population Report*, p. 60, No. 83 (Washington, D.C.: Government Printing Office, July 1972)

The Nixon people aren't the least bit upset by their lack of progress. They just claim progress and give you figures to prove it. Thus they claim that, indeed, nonwhites gained during the Nixon reign, pointing out that in 1967 nonwhite income was 62.75 percent of white income whereas in 1971 nonwhites had crept up to 62.91 percent—ooh-ha—forgetting to point out that people don't spend percentages at the store, they spend dollars, and that if both groups are increasing in incomes the percentages are likely to *appear* to narrow while the *real* differences between the two go up.

As for women, how did they do, compared with men? They failed again. A statistical presentation by head of family income would not be appropriate for men-women comparisons since many women with high-paying jobs would be calculated as part of a family income with a male head of household. A comparison of persons in prestigious jobs might prove illustrative. The following table provides that contrast.

TABLE 4
Men and women in professional and managerial positions 1960, 1965, 1968, 1969, 1970, 1971 (numbers in millions)

Year	Men	Women	Differences
1960	10.7	3.9	6.8
1965	11.8	4.4	7.4
1968	13.0	5.1	7.9
1969	13.5	5.3	8.2
1970	13.8	5.6	8.2
1971	13.9	5.8	8.1

SOURCE: *Statistical Abstract*, 1971, 1972.

The interesting aspect of the above statistics is that the Kennedy-Johnson years were *not* years that offered gains to women when compared to men. However, opportunities in status positions leaped during the sixties for both men and women. Almost 3 million more men and a million and a half more women gained professional or managerial occupations between the time Eisenhower left office and Nixon was inaugurated. This growth slowed perceptibly for men once Nixon took office. For women the increase did not slacken as much, but again those positions are limited and even here may have reflected growth in a few fields only, particularly nursing and teaching. The teaching field, unless there are changes in governmental policy, has crested, and nursing, while improved in prestige and income, continues to lag behind the emoluments offered the male-dominated physician status. In 1970 there were almost 50 percent more registered nurses than was the case in 1960; their numbers are likely to increase by comparable amounts in the next decade (*Manpower Report of the President,* 1972, p. 133). Projections on other fields such as engineering, math, the social sciences, and educational administration do not present anywhere near as rosy a picture of declining inequality between the sexes.

Bear in mind that the amount of money the president has to play with is considerable. President Nixon has announced that he intends to keep the federal spending down to $250 billion in the fiscal year 1973–1974. Two hundred fifty billion dollars is a bunch of money, it could create a lot of decent paying jobs. Over 31 million positions paying an average of $8,000 could be created with such an amount; that is more than a third of the people currently working. But this is not likely to happen. What is likely is that the federal budget will increase and the people directly employed because of it will decrease—a safe conclusion based on recent history. As the following table indicates, Richard Nixon does less with the federal dollar than any of our most recent presidents.

With Presidents Kennedy and Johnson the cost per federal job increased about 3.7 percent per year, with Mr. Nixon the increase is almost 10 percent per year.

TABLE 5

Federal government employed and federal government expenditures, 1962–1971

Year	Federal government employment (in millions)	Federal government expenditures (in billions of dollars)	Cost per job (in thousands of dollars)	Increase in cost per year (in thousands of dollars)
1962	8.4	67.5	8.0	.2
1963	8.4	68.7	8.2	.2
1964	8.2	69.9	8.5	.3
1965	8.1	71.9	8.9	.4
1966	8.7	83.3	9.6	.7
1967	9.6	96.6	10.1	.5
1968	9.8	105.4	10.8	.7
1969	9.3	106.3	11.4	.6
1970	8.4	105.5	12.6	1.2
1971	7.6	97.2	14.5	1.9

SOURCE: *Manpower Report of the President* (Washington, D.C.: Government Printing Office), pgs. 283–1284.

a Includes employment in private industry, civilian and military government service, and employment in government enterprises (e.g.,-postal service).

b Includes purchase from private industry, compensation for civilian, military, and government enterprise employees.

c Excludes government enterprise employees and compensation. In recent years, however, exclusion of such work raised this average cost per job, so 1971 is an understatement of *cost per job.*

One reason the costs of government services are so high is

that much of the money is given to the private sector of the economy in the form of contracts. It turns out to be *far* more expensive to generate employment by subsidizing some private business than by the government itself hiring the workers. The cost to the government for a *subsidized* worker in profit-making ventures is about twice that of a person actually working for the governmental agencies. Extending beyond this is the *nature* of government employment. In 1970 more than four-fifths of the money for federal authorized employment in the private sector was in military matters, whereas only (ahem) 63.5 percent of the monies the federal government spent for hiring people was in military-related work. There is a strange cost relation between military and nonmilitary work. In the private sector, military work is more expensive than nondefense activities, and the reverse holds true for federal employment. This relation stems from the traditional low wages of enlisted men—but, with plans for an all-voluntary army, the cost functions of soldier pay and retirement benefit are projected to rise significantly.

I object to the term *voluntary army* as used by the Nixon phrasemongers. I stand for a true volunteer army: when a person wants to fight, he brings his own equipment. When he wants to travel to do it, he brings his own transportation—otherwise, he can't come or go. Such an approach to the military would cut down the costs and people would, for the first time, fight only for fun and not for profit.

All well and interesting, but what has this to do with Richard Nixon?

As the following table shows, with Richard Nixon the costs of labor, both privately subsidized and publicly employed, go up markedly.

TABLE 6

Contracts with private industry compared with federal government employment cost per job, 1962–1970

Year	PRIVATE CONTRACTS			FEDERAL GOVERNMENT		
	Persons employed (millions)	Dollars spent (millions)	Cost/job (thousands)	Persons employed (millions)	Dollars spent (millions)	Cost/job (thousands)
1962	3.7	39.1	10.6	5.3	28.4	5.4
1963	3.9	39.0	10.0	5.2	29.7	5.7
1964	3.7	38.0	10.3	5.2	31.9	6.1
1965	3.5	38.4	11.0	5.4	33.5	6.2
1966	3.6	45.2	12.6	6.0	38.1	6.4
1967	4.1	54.8	13.4	6.4	41.8	6.5
1968	4.2	59.3	14.1	6.5	46.1	7.1
1969	3.7	57.0	15.4	6.5	49.2	7.6
1970	3.3	52.4	15.9	6.0	53.1	8.8
NONDEFENSE SPENDING						
1962	.8	6.1	7.6	1.4	9.5	6.8
1963	1.3	7.2	5.5	1.4	10.4	7.4
1964	1.1	8.4	7.6	1.4	11.2	8.0
1965	1.0	9.5	9.5	1.6	12.0	7.5
1966	.8	9.3	11.6	1.8	13.0	7.2
1967	.9	9.9	11.0	1.8	14.0	7.8
1968	.8	11.2	14.0	1.8	15.6	8.7
1969	.8	10.8	13.5	1.8	16.7	9.3
1970	.7	10.3	14.7	1.8	19.4	10.8

SOURCE: *Manpower Report of the President, 1972* (Washington, D.C.: Government Printing Office), Tables G-18, G-11, pp. 283–284.

It would seem—at least from a quick glance at figures— that Mr. Nixon has cut back on governmental support of business. In 1970 almost $5 billion fewer were let to industry in the form of contracts and this was almost $7 billion less than the high established in the last year Lyndon Johnson was in office. Thus it would appear Richard Nixon is less a believer in socialism for the rich than LBJ. That could be, because Mr. Johnson clearly was not opposed to helping the rich get richer, but the difference was more of style than intent. Under Johnson private industry got more contracts; with Nixon private industry got their money outright in the form of gifts. (I will get to that in a few paragraphs.) However, the key issue should not be lost or obscured. When it came to use of federal dollars for employment under the Nixon administration, the value received for the public dollar declined—something which Mr. Nixon never bothers to reconcile with his alleged opposition to inflation. Perhaps government costs could best be understood by the way Mr. Nixon conducts his own affairs.

One person who doesn't believe that he should do much for himself is our president Richard Nixon. No president ever demanded so much help and his own professed helplessness partially explains the bloating of employment costs in the federal government. Thomas E. Cronin describes the increase in presidential staff in an article entitled "The Swelling of the Presidency" (*Saturday Review of the Society*, February 1973). Thus:

> There are no official figures on the size of the Presidential Establishment, and standard body counts vary widely depending on who is and who is not included in the count, but by one frequently used reckoning, between five and six thousand people work for the President of the United States. Payroll and maintenance costs for this staff run between $100 million and $150 million a year. (These

figures include the Office of Economic Opportunity [OEO], which is an Executive Office agency and employs two thousand people, but not the roughly fifteen thousand-man Central Intelligence Agency, although that, too, is directly responsible to the Chief Executive.) These "White House" workers have long since outgrown the White House itself and now occupy not only two wings of the executive mansion but three nearby high-rise office buildings as well.

The expansion of the Presidential Establishment, it should be emphasized, is by no means only a phenomenon of the Nixon years. The number of employees under the President has been growing steadily since the early 1900s when only a few dozen people served in the White House entourage, at a cost of less than a few hundred thousand dollars annually. Congress's research arm, the Congressional Research Service, has compiled a count that underlines in particular the accelerated increase in the last two decades. This compilation shows that between 1954 and 1971 the number of presidential advisers has grown from 25 to 45, the White House staff from 266 to 600, and the Executive Office staff from 1,175 to 5,395.

The announced cuts of White House staff in January 1973 affected transfer of Executive Office staff—not his own personal group of advisers. There was no mention of a cutback to one White House, for example, as an economy measure.

So much for government employment, but that's hardly the whole story since the $105 billion reflected in government employment and employment in contracts with private industry amount to only 53 percent of the $197 billion federal government outlays of 1970. Where did the rest of the money go? The following table tells that story.

Examine how each of the outlays affects work in the United States. The single largest expenditure of the federal government, aside from military, is social insurance (old age assistance, medical insurance, unemployment insurance, etc.). The federal budget for 1970 was almost $46 billion for such services. This would appear to be a humane usage of public

TABLE 7
Federal government budget outlays, 1970

Source of expenditure Total	Amount in billions of dollars
Government Employment (all sources)	53
Employment (Government Contracts)	52
Social Insurance	43
Public Aid	8
Health and Medical Programs	4
School Meals	2
Veterans Benefits	8
Education	5
Housing	5
Direct Subsidies	11
Interest on Debt	16
Impounding	—5

SOURCE: *Pocket Data Book*, U.S.A. 1971. (Washington, D.C., U.S. Department of Commerce, Bureau of Census.)

ª Allocations have been adjusted to take into account the salaries and wages paid to persons working for the various agencies.

monies. The misery of suffering people during the Great Depression inspired such legislation and, given the exigency of the time, little else could have been done, but now such approaches to social problems have outlived their usefulness and, rather than expiring, have grown to huge unmanageable bureaucracies. Social insurance programs fail to achieve their purposes primarily because there has been so little analysis of the impact that social insurance by itself has on work. The net result is that service declines as the price goes up. This result is either ignored or not understood by the Nixon administration. It focuses on increasing the money for the service while simultaneously cutting back on persons employed in human service, which *must* cause inflation.

Understand how this happens. Many billions of dollars are provided selected individuals who are, because of their poverty, age, or infirmity, in undesirable bargaining positions. The monies they receive add to aggregate consumer demand, which means there is an inflationary tug on the economy. Here transfer payments act just like military spending. The problem is that, while government has assisted in increasing aggregate demand, it has not assisted in developing a commensurate array of goods and services. Here again transfer payments are just like military expenditures. (The average citizen cannot buy or eat a B-52, which he has paid for and received wages to build, service, and fly.) In fact, government has ensured throughout all its behaviors that the goods and services will not be there. Therein lies a major dilemma of our society.

Take medicine as a specific example: with the passage of Medicare legislation, 20 million people could obtain medical services many never had before—this led to a huge increase in demand. How about the supply? Not everybody can legally call himself a doctor. The government licenses M.D.s (with the assistance of the established medical association). To become a licensed M.D., a person must successfully complete medical training, most of the cost of which is borne by the government. But government has not kept pace in support of activities that would increase medical practitioners or revised its licensing procedures so that new services could be initiated—so what have we got? We got a lot more expensive medicine! The chief beneficiary of medical insurance is the M.D. who wasn't doing so bad prior to all this insurance. Who is the loser? The client and the taxpayer, who has to pay more and more for less and less. Again, figures are illustrative.

In 1969 the average M.D. in the United States made $44,550 (most of which he was able to keep because of expensively designed tax shelters). Four years before he was drawing down almost $12,000 less—$28,960. In 1969 there were 338,000 licensed doctors in the United States; four years earlier there were 305,000. Between 1965 and 1969, income for M.D.s rose 40.0 percent while their numbers increased only 10 percent.

The trend in medicine is likely to continue and is only indicative of the mentality of our president. Medical costs will rise unless there is both an increase in available doctors and a reorganization of services.* If 40 percent more doctors were in the field in 1969, it is likely that their increased income would be only 10 percent in four years and, unless something like *that* happens, it is pure demagoguery to talk about inflation control. A 40 percent increase in M.D.s in four years would increase by 90,000 the numbers now working in such a lofty field and would also make possible the absorption of far more poor, more women, more minorities into medical care. President Nixon, throughout his political career, has consistently opposed programs which would increase the delivery of medical services.

The medical mess has come about because government has interceded to increase demand without providing for increased services. Education operates differently and very imperfectly, but provides an example of how government could at least keep some control over the process. In education, government is involved in both sides of the equation, providing means by which demand has been increased (college financial assistance programs, increasing the educational budget, etc.) but also directly employing the teacher. There is a lot wrong with this system but, in terms of providing employment at far less inflationary prices, it beats hell out of giving money to the people and then making sure they have nothing to buy. In 1965 the average elementary and secondary school teacher made $6,200 a year. Four years later, this

* See Arthur Pearl and Frank Riessman, *New Careers for the Poor* (New York: Free Press, 1964), for some suggested reorganizations of medical care.

127

was increased by $1,800 (that's a sizable increase of 29 percent, but the teacher's actual gain seems piddling when contrasted with that of the M.D. In 1965 the teacher was making $22,800 less a year than a doctor. In 1969 the teacher was making $32,598 less a year than a doctor! The teacher salary increases reflected a need to catch up with inflation; the doctor was one of the causes of it. Mr. Nixon is on the side of the doctor.

Some of you might argue that government providing services is a form of socialism—a popular argument among people who know nothing about either socialism or decent human services—but if you define creation of services as socialistic, then Richard Nixon qualifies as half a socialist in his support of increased demand, and if you insist that half a socialist is better than none (or all), I just want to know which half he is. I have my suspicions.

Now to the direct subsidy boondoggle. Mr. Nixon loves to give our money away to big business, another group which he is not asking to help themselves. (Yes he is, he invites them to help themselves to more and more wealth and then throws the power of government behind them.) In 1970, $10.6 billion were given away in direct subsidies. The following table indicates the trend over the past few years.

TABLE 8
Federal subsidies programs, net expenditures 1960, 1965, 1967, 1968, 1969, 1970 (in billions of dollars)

	1960	1965	1967	1968	1969	1970
Total	5.7	6.6	6.9	6.9	8.3	10.7
Agriculture	3.9	4.2	3.6	3.5	5.0	5.5
Business	1.4	1.6	2.1	2.1	1.8	2.3
Labor	.3	.5	.6	.6	.7	.9
Homeowners and tenants		.1	.3	.3	.2	1.6
Other	.1	.2	.3	.4	.5	.4

SOURCE: *Pocket Data Book*, U.S.A. (Washington, D.C.: U.S. Department of Commerce, Bureau of Census, 1971), p. 86.

When one looks at giveaway programs, the direction of government is quite clear. Under Nixon them what gots—gets. The increase in federal subsidies rose very slowly during the Kennedy-Johnson years—less than 6 per cent per year. In one short year that increased more than fourfold under Richard Nixon. The effect of subsidies served to increase inflation and reduce employment. In agriculture, the subsidy program further jeopardized the most vulnerable of our workers, the farm laborer, while forcing food prices to jump nearly out of sight.

Farm subsidies, representing the cruelest of all giveaway programs, are much like transfer payment programs. They emerge today as a corrupt reincarnation of once progressive governmental intervention. The original concept, developed by now much maligned Secretary of Agriculture Henry A. Wallace, was designed to prop up falling farm prices during the midst of a terrible depression. The beneficiaries were the large numbers of impoverished small farmers. The propping of prices remains, but now it is in the midst of inflation and worldwide hunger. The beneficiaries are no longer the small farmers. Now the huge agribusiness firms profit (as well as other rich looking for tax shelters) while the small farmer has virtually been exterminated with almost the same efficiency as his predecessor on the land—the American Indian. The net result is a continued decline in persons working in agriculture, an increased threat to the environment because of monocultural large-scale farming, pesticides, and manufactured fertilizers, and a continued increase in food prices. It is a policy in which everyone suffers and only a handful benefit. Because of this considerable insanity, we discover in the first week of 1973 that prices have risen more dramatically in the last months of the Nixon first term than at any time in the previous twenty-five years, that food costs have skyrocketed and that Secretary of Agriculture Butz proposes a modest cutback in the farm subsidy program. If there were true concern for inflation, government support would go to the beleaguered small farmer and devastated farm worker. But that doesn't happen, sucker—and *you* paid.

The giveaway mentality of Richard Nixon continues to accelerate. He has given away the Post Office—again, much heralded, but with no perceptible progress—he has given to business job training and educational innovation. It is strange he hasn't hit on the logical extension to all of this; he hasn't contracted out the military in its entirety. If four years ago he had established a performance-based contract with some profit-making corporation—for example, the Mafia—at, let's say, $1,000 for every dead "enemy"—why in two years at the most we could have wiped out *all* of North and South Vietnam and almost everybody else we don't like.

If the president *does* decide to turn the military over to private enterprise, remember: You heard it here *first!*

There is yet another way the president influences work and that is with his tax programs. When he is not giving money away to the rich, he is using his influence as president to make sure that they, his closest friends and political supporters, are not required to foot their fair share of government cost. For that group only death has become inevitable.

Tax expert Stanley S. Surrey, professor of tax law at Harvard Law School and author of *Federal Income Taxation*, succinctly summarized the Nixon approach to taxation:

> The high income investor can join partnership in oil, real estate, cattle, farms or equipment leasing businesses that produce large "tax losses"—such as an investor's expenses for feeding his cattle—which are losses only in the eye of the tax law. In the investor's own accounts the expenses are outlays on which he hopes eventually to make money. Meanwhile, on his tax return the "losses" can be deducted to offset income from other sources, thereby making much of the other income nontaxable.
>
> There is something terribly amiss when, in order to provide low-income housing for the shelter of the poor, we at the same time shelter tax millionaires. We permit investors

an accelerated depreciation on buildings far in excess of the real decline in the buildings' values. As a result of this loophole, and others like it, persons with actual incomes in the hundreds of thousands, even millions, either pay no income tax or pay at a rate less than that of semiskilled construction workers. This is an offense to our sense of fairness and decency. . . .

The same criticisms hold true for corporations. We know that by law the tax rate on major corporations is 48 per cent, and yet the overall rate they pay is, in effect, only 35 per cent. Indeed, for some corporations the effective rate is still lower, sometimes even zero. Many a tax-escape path can be found by companies—quick and excessive depreciation, overly generous depletion allowances, untaxed profits derived abroad, and reduced taxes on income from exports.

. . . The Nixon administration has not made a single tax-reform proposal on its own that would end a single tax preference or close a single loophole. . . . Instead of backing reform, this administration has taken the path of more tax incentives for business—indefinite deferral of taxes on half of all income from exports (DISC) and even faster tax-saving write-offs for machinery. Each incentive has created a new tax escape (*Saturday Review of the Society*, November 1972).

The Richard Nixon approach to taxation has impact on employment in very destructive ways. The favored treatment of the goods-producing segments of our economy means that the work required to make, warehouse, transport, and sell "things" comes at the expense of human service. It also means that the environment is endangered by depletion of oil resources and nonreplenishable metal. It also means that wealth is accrued in the hands of a few who, because of their means, can launch advertising campaigns to convince us to buy things that are obviously not needed for quality life. The concentration of wealth in the hands of the few means also that poverty continues to plague many and that distribution of poverty continues to deny work opportunity to persons on the basis of sex, income, or skin color. These are inescapable conclusions and no amount of rhetoric or double-talk or posturing will wash these truths away. But that's not all the devastation that comes with a Nixon presidency. There is more.

The special privileges given the rich plus an unfair burden on the middle-income person forces on this group a Hobson's choice. Either they pay more taxes or cut back on public services (which means cut back on employment, which means cut back on taxpayers). Richard Nixon, on presentation of his first postelection budget to Congress on January 29, 1973, announced the elimination of many social service programs including the Emergency Employment Service, which had at modest costs provided employment for 280,000 people in vital services in state and local agencies. Mr. Nixon justified all of this by asserting to Congress that alternatives to his plans would lead to "high taxes, higher interest, renewed inflation, or all three."

Bushwah! *His* programs have led to all these undesirable conditions. *His* programs will continue to worsen the economy, but reiterations of the hold-the-line line do serve to make the average taxpayer more conservative, because that taxpayer is made to feel that he or she alone has to pay for any increase in government service.

The tax privileges offered the rich affect work in the private sector. The beneficiaries of the tax loophole used their monies to create labor-saving devices (which is one way to obtain tax benefits) and thereby reduce employment possibilities, increase use of oil and metals, and increase their hold over the political structure by an ever-mounting concentration of wealth. The entrenched economic power is used to ensure inequitable tax policies which increase labor-saving devices, further undermining the environment, making even more powerful the already superpowerful.

And so it goes—

And soon it may be all gone.

The single most comprehensive insight into Nixon thinking is found in the New Economic Policy announced in August 1971. Until the president came forth with this policy, the nation was drifting: both unemployment *and* inflation were rising, there was little direction except in the form of vetoes from the president, the national debt was at an all-time high, and the United States was undergoing a period of chronic unfavorable balance of payments. The increase in the national debt was particularly embarrassing to the president (or should have been if anyone bothered to notice) because fiscal year 1970–1971 was the year that Nixon proclaimed as the first in which he fully applied his budgetary principles. So, New Economic Policy was trumpeted to the world. It had four parts:

Part 1 called for a control over wages and prices

Part 2 called for an increase in tariff and other regulations to protect home industries

Part 3 created tax holidays for the private employer—for example, removal of excise taxes on new automobiles

Part 4 ordered a cutback on government services to pay for the loss in taxes.

The sum total of the New Economic Policy was to seriously cripple job development in the United States. The cutback on governmental services cut back on vital needs *and* employment. The tax holidays supported the highly technical private goods producing segment of our economy which, as will be shown, is a poor job provider.

But there was another aspect of the president's employment policy which is as important as unemployment itself. This is the impact of work on the environment. Mr. Nixon pursues a policy that eats nonreplenishable resources (metals and oil), and leaving the world buried in its residue (pollution) while he actively opposes support of work compatible with nature. As I have commented elsewhere,

Human Service is ecologically defensible work because the activities depend primarily on human energy. The doctor, teacher, entomologist, portrait painter and youth gang worker all rely fundamentally on the energy produced from the calories that they eat. The products of work consumption, carbon dioxide and other waste materials, if dispersed, contribute to the life processes of other living organisms.

... human service is labor intensive and can be used to extend and repair the environment—something *no* capital intensive activity can be made to do.*

Hold it! What's so bad about using our tax dollars to subsidize private enterprise? Well, obviously, when the public subsidizes industries they are no longer private—but that's not the central issue. The key point is that such support doesn't create many jobs. The money goes primarily to the larger corporations. The chief beneficiaries of the New Economic Policy were automobile manufacturers and, therefore, oil companies. Six out of the 10 largest corporations are directly tied to automobiles. The top ten corporations in 1971 accounted for 11.3 per cent of the Gross National Product, and they hired only 3.0 million people or 3.8 percent of the persons working.†

This means that, in effect, each worker was accountable for $39,000 of economic activity. A handsome proportion of that $39,000 was government subsidized. We can do a lot better than that with our money, and it's the president who needs some discipline—it is he who is profligate with both our dollars and our environment.*

But hold it for another cotton-picking minute—Democrats by and large and particularly well-known liberal economists

---

* "A Human Service Society—An Ecological Approach," Riessman, Nixon, and Gartner (ed.) , in *Public Service Employment* (New York: Praeger, 1973) .
† (In *Fortune* magazine, May 1972.)
* For a more complete explanation of the point, see Pearl, *op. cit.*

like Galbraith and Samuelson welcomed Nixon's New Economic Policy, complaining only that it took him too long to get there, didn't they?

Yep! And therein lies a large part of the problem—Democrats and particularly labor-oriented Democrats are as confused about work as is the president. They tend to opt for inceased governmental insurance programs and, while they argue for increased services, they tend to support entrenched bureaucracies which are both inefficient and impersonal. The need for a society of, for, and by humans escapes the descendants of the New Deal almost to the extent that such a concept eludes economic fundamentalists. The labor-liberal Democrat has been an unabashed supporter of the new technology and has not recognized the devastation that this technological society has wrought on the distribution of power, the alienation of humans from each other, and the erosion of quantity and quality of work. The lack of vision of what a world should look like has led to selfish and sectarian demands for more on the part of both those on top and those in the middle. With those kinds of demands, guess who is going without dinner?

Enough already. You have established Nixon's responsibility for slackening employment, environmentally destructive work, maintaining job bias, helping the rich, and undermining of public service, but you haven't said anything about his role in worker dissatisfaction. Pray, how could he have effected that?

The role of the president as chief public educator cannot be minimized. He and his staff constantly flood the media with notions that influence all thinking. One of Nixon's unending themes is a devout faith in the work ethic. On Labor Day of 1971, shortly after enunciating the New Economic Policy, he proclaimed that "it was alive and well in the

United States." As I have said, people want to believe their president—it is extremely disquieting not to be able to believe him. There wasn't a smidgen of evidence to support such a statement. *All* the evidence was to the contrary—worker morale was low everywhere. In fact, the president—through the secretary of health, education, and welfare—sponsored an official look into worker happiness. The conclusion published a month *after* Mr. Nixon's reelection was that the work ethic was ill and in hiding in the United States. The report speaks for itself:

> Many of the nation's 82 million workers hate their jobs and their unhappiness is causing major social problems, a new government sponsored report said yesterday.
> "Worker discontent is measured by declines in physical and mental health, family stability and community participation, and an increase in social and political alienation, aggression, delinquency and drug and alcohol addiction," said the task force report.
> Its major recommendation is to redesign dull, repetitive jobs to give workers more say in what they do, which many of them put even ahead of wages in importance (AP report, December 22, 1972).

The HEW report is characteristic of a schizophrenic quality of Nixon leadership. On the one hand, the staff sponsor reports indicate great dissatisfaction with work but, on the other hand, he designs economic policies that maintain high unemployment rates, meaning that employers are under no pressure to redesign jobs and that labor, threatened by job insecurities, are in no position to recommend such alternatives because in the redesign they are likely to be shuffled out. Nixon's policies lend support to huge private bureaucracies and give buying power with no provision of services, which makes any work redesign extremely difficult if not impossible.

Finally, his silence about work design—coming, I suspect, because he knows so little about work in the sense that most of us have had to experience it—creates the vacuum that a rush of outmoded nonsolutions fill. All of this not only leads to worker dissatisfaction, but also leads to dissatisfaction of the patient, the client, and the customer.

How did Nixon get away with all of this?

It is not too difficult to understand how Nixon was re-elected; even though the work situation was deteriorating, he rode triumphantly to a second term by resonating with prevalent myths and striking out at discredited myths. In the absence of enlightenment, myths take hold; human beings searching for meaning and order in their lives will cling desperately to superstition to explain what otherwise seems unfathomable. These are the myths Nixon responded to and possibly even shared—which might make him more of a fool than a fooler:

1. Anyone can get a job if only he or she tries hard enough.
2. People advance to the top on the basis of ability—which explains why the rich are rich and the poor, poor.
3. Kids are spoiled rotten today and want everything handed them on a silver platter (an attitude derived from permissive institutions like the school and social-ist-oriented governments).
4. Jobs are created by Big Business and therefore tax privileges should be given to them (and, if we don't they might get mad and throw people out of work in a fit of pique).
5. Government employment is basically bad because it encourages laziness and inefficiency and is a perilous step in the direction of socialism.
6. Government should practice austerity through balanced budgets and minimum taxation and, if jobs are lost because of this, the gain for a free economy is worth it.

Mr. Nixon has, throughout his political career, been associated with the right-wing myths—these are the right myths to become attached to politically, they have been carefully cultivated and fertilized by all our educational and propaganda institutions. That's what our children learn in schools and our adults on television, in newspapers and magazines—in fact, almost everywhere.

The ability of those who really want it to get a job is believed by every age group. A Gallup Poll in the summer of 1972 found all populations support such a myth, including 60 percent of the college youth who, for the first time in thirty years, were scuffling for jobs.

A Gallup Poll in the winter of 1972 found all income, age, and educational groups favoring Mr. Nixon's fiscal plans to cut back on social programs.

The disparagement of public service employment is a strange myth; during the depression such work was for many literally the only alternative to starvation, and yet the notion that such work is bad is regenerated. It is almost as if people trying to eradicate from their minds hard and desperate days flail out at everything associated with them. It is even more curious that Mr. Nixon should be opposed to public employment since it is about the only work he's ever had.

The data ticked off in the preceding pages should embarrass holders of right-wing myths, but very few of these "true believers" are likely to be convinced. They want something substantial to replace superstition. In the pages that follow some suggestions for change will be presented, but it is to be understood that myths die hard. Right-wing myths are particularly dangerous because they hang on without the slightest attachment to fact. They are sustained to a large extent by rejection of other myths. Myths don't die naturally. They resist killing because they provide psychological mucilage—they tie the loose ends of our life together. They justify selfishness, lack of social concern, even crime.

The right wing takes advantage of the discredited left-wing superstitions—among which can be found:

1. Work is no longer a legitimate concern since machines can do what most people can do and do it better (ergo, people who still think about work can't get over their Calvinistic need for suffering).
2. Elimination of private capital is an essential prerequisite for any significant work reform.
3. Every person in the United States should have a guaranteed income whether he or she works or not.
4. Government spending on welfare and poverty programs is better than doing nothing at all.

The left of America gave through their own fuzziness a legitimacy to Richard Nixon that he could not construct for himself. They didn't even need to be distorted, they did that for themselves.

The most devastating myth conjured up in the 1960s was that income without work was both desirable and possible. It is neither. Income without work implies that machines will do what humans used to do. Thus the human becomes ever more dependent (perhaps, as Jacques Ellul says in his book *The Technological Society*, totally subservient) on infernal devices which at one time were only an adjunct to human activity. Whenever humans are replaced by machines, this means that ever more quickly the rapidly depleting resources such as oil and metals will be totally devoured. How would you like to be on the L.A. freeway the day the world runs out of gasoline?

Work turned over to machines *must* be impersonal. The human beings must adjust to the capacities of the machine. Assembly line work is both dreary and taxing, services provided by machines allow for no provision for exceptional problems—and each of us, in things that really matter, is a very special case. For example, I have tried for fully five years to get from the American Express Company $63 *they* owe *me*, but the computer doesn't recognize such requests and my form response is always that my card has been canceled and that dire things will happen to me if I persist in using what I haven't had in five years.

Work turned over to machines places unreasonable burdens on the human worker and furthers the illusion that many human beings—particularly minorities, other poor, youth, and women—are unemployable. The myth of unemployability is fostered by the potential expensive mischief that untrained and otherwise suspect people can cause when placed near costly machinery or electronic paraphernalia. The reduction of job growth that comes as a result of automation and rationalization of work limits work opportunities and permits employers to impose "higher standards" as prerequisites for entry positions for advancement. The lack of work opportunities in turn lends support to the myth of unemployability. There are virtually no unemployable people, a fact that every emergency drives home. During World War II, for example, welfare claims fell to near zero, and work was adapted to fit the needs of the handicapped, women, and so on.

Work turned over to machines increases the power that those who run the machines have over the individual and also the wealth of those who run or control the machines. That wealth in turn is translated into more political power. Work turned over to machines generates vital secrets shared by only a privileged elite and leaves the vast majority ignorant of the workings of the society in which they live.

Is it any wonder that many many people would react to those portents and opt for the simple life myths of Richard Nixon?

The myth of a workers' paradise through the overthrow of capitalism persists among an ever more isolated segment of our society, to the delight of those who are in the driver's seat. Those in control are happy that the belief is isolated, but they are also pleased that the residual myth remains. If there were no reds to bait, it would be more difficult to ride to power through red-baiting (and where indeed would Richard Nixon be today without red-baiting?).

Those who harp on the evils of capitalism must somehow reconcile their belief structure with the political trends in the United States. With one-third of the popular vote in 1920, and while still in prison, Eugene Debs managed to get almost one million votes—and it has been downhill for almost any variety of socialist since then.

The myth of miracles through elimination of capitalism itself needs to be reexamined in this, the ninetieth anniversary of Karl Marx's death. One truth cannot be treated superficially, and this is that the elimination of private enterprise has not, in the numerous experiments that have had a chance to flower in the twentieth century, created "workers' paradises" anywhere. Socialists who admit such failings are like football coaches, lauding the idea while decrying the execution. That won't wash. The problem goes deeper than flawed leadership or revisionistic ideology. The worker paradise myth remains a myth because the utopia left out the nature, distribution, and all other attributes of work in the current technical world. In many ways most socialist utopias are technological wonderlands. Most followers of Karl Marx believe in infinite nature; they are unreconstructed Rousseaus believing that human beings, if uncorrupted by grasping, grubby wealth accruers, will remain forever noble. But, mostly, socialists are naïve; they are removed from political relevance not only because the population they wish to influence has been fed a steady diet of antisocialist indoctrination, but also because they have removed *themselves* from any popular appeal. Socialists do not relate to where people are—at work, in political activity, in culture, in leisure, and in very personal intimacies; thus the "socialists" become "setups" for political opportunists like Richard Nixon.

Those who believe that elimination of private industry is essential for universal quality life must, if they are to play any constructive political role in the future, translate that proposal into concrete visions: What will be the work of people? Where will they live? How will they transport themselves? What will be their leisure? If there is to be some relief from the oppressive current bureaucracies, how will political and work activities be organized?

And to accomplish such a program, what are the first steps? When they do that, socialists are likely to shed a myth or two.

There is a particularly corruptive notion among some alleged radicals—namely, that economic revolution must precede any significant reform of work. This is a complete and total copout. There can be no large-scale change in economic and political structure without a majority of persons consciously wanting it and a large percentage of persons actively working for it—and this can't happen until persons are reached at the level of immediate concern.

Related to the notion that machines can do work is the idea that income detached from work can be given to large numbers of persons with no apparent negative effect on the economy.

What is ignored is that income must be generated somewhere. It has to be drawn from some reservoir of wealth. If the utility is gained from sophisticated technology through automated production and services, the impact on the environment is in the form of depleted fossil fuels and minerals. If the utility is gained from human endeavor, a few have to bear the burden for the many, an extremely inequitable arrangement, one generating an enormous pull toward inflation through increase of buying power without a comparable incease in goods and services. In either instance, those given income will always be in an unfavorable wealth and power condition vis-à-vis those who work and those who own or control the production of goods and services. The interests of those who have income and don't work are at cross-purposes with those who work for their income. The former wants as much of the income as he or she can get. This can come about only by increasing taxation and, the way things are, the persons who have to pay the taxes are those already overtaxed —the average working persons. This fundamental disagreement leads to the disruption of political alliances which Richard Nixon used to full advantage. McGovern's stand for a guaranteed income was his second most costly political error (the first was allowing Nixon to steal the peace issue).

Yet another myth of the left is the belief that any program designed to spend money on the poor is a good program (almost the reverse of "What's good for General Motors is good for the country"). This is not true! Most of the Great Society consisted of bad programs; very few were good. The preponderance were bad because they assumed poverty resulted from inadequacies in the poor; thus the "educationally handicapped" were compensated for nonexistent deficiencies to the tune of $2 billion or so a year, ghetto youths were transported thousands of miles to unfriendly rural camps to be trained for nonexistent jobs, little children were given head starts to remediate alleged environmental deficits they had received from their parents. The programs were bad because the insufficient funds were deflected away from the poor to nonpoor teachers, social workers, and so on. The programs were bad because operating outside of the important, well-endowed established agencies, they deflected attention away from real sources of inequality, thus adding to the illusion of progress. The lack of connection of good society programs to political strength made them setups for Richard Nixon and his aides to demolish with exaggerated charges of corruption and inefficiencies and other things which Richard Nixon knows best.

The myths emanating from the vision killers, who like to think themselves in the middle of the extremes, are also devastating. These are the myths of the "realists," who argue in effect that any true changes in life conditions are beyond human capacity and are the figments of romantics. Thus they proclaim that:

- full employment is inflationary
- work activities require vigorous standards, which is why minorities are excluded from important positions
- it is distinctly possible that many nonwhites are genetically incapable of anything more than marginal contributions to the work world
- schools cannot play a useful role in reducing inequality of work opportunities
- war budgets are not damaging to domestic salubrity

Probably the most widely held destructive myth about work is that full employment is not economically desirable. The postulated Phillips relationship between full employment and inflation has been a salient argument for policies which slowed down the economy and increased unemployment. Elevating the question whether full employment is inflationary to paramount importance reveals the lack of vision among economists as a group.

Visionary economists would be asking how could full employment be noninflationary? Such a question would require an examination of public education which stimulates appetites for goods; established procedures for determination of wages; regulations which influence price systems; tax policies which affect buying power; proscription of inflationary practices and activities designed to increase the supply of goods and services.

Merely observing that current economic policies produce an association between low employment rates and reduction of the worth of the dollar is not an outstanding scientific accomplishment. Hypothesizing the cause of the relationship still wouldn't amount to much. The essence of true science involves proposals which resolve the problem.

Inflation does not have to accompany full employment. Persons can be educated to want no more than they need. Wages *can* be regulated to keep prices in bounds without disrupting democratic procedures, a tax strategy *can* be implemented reducing aggregate demand for goods, laws *can* be established prohibiting price increases, and services *can* be created to keep pace with aggregate demands. The vision killers are strangely quiet when it comes to proposing *anything* constructive.

Structural unemployment is another hobby horse that vision killers love to ride. They prate about meritocracies and the need to screen persons carefully before they are allowed into sensitive work positions or universities which prepare people for prestigious work. The question of the validity of admissions criteria is given short shrift and charges of bias are summarily dismissed as expressions of "naïve environmentalism" by "incurable romantics." The credentials system of our society is maintained by those who possess the requirements for employment and they make themselves impervious to serious criticism or suggested reform. It is clear that the procedures currently used to develop professional staff *do not* produce quality service nor do those procedures reduce unequal opportunities for the poor, women, or non-white minorities.

In effect, the vision killers become apologists for racism, classism, and sexism. They become the wardens of mind control. Thus they try to overwhelm any proposals for drastic reform. The role they play is deftly described by S. M. Miller and Ronnie Steinberg Ratner:

> If manpower programs failed to deliver decent jobs for trainees, then unemployment must result from the pathology of the trainees. If educational expenditures for the poor get frittered away by recalcitrant and money-hungry schools, then there must be something basically and irretrievably deficient about Black children. If poor people don't save for that rainy day, it can't be because they lack sufficient income for current, let alone longer-run, needs.*

After every halfhearted attempt to improve the economic condition of nonwhites in the United States, vision-killing liberals resurrect the notion that perhaps whites are genetically superior to nonwhites. The latest such advocate is Arthur Jensen, University of California educational psychologist, who insists that perhaps blacks are where they are because constitutionally they are capable of no better. Other "liberals" discover other deficits—lack of intellectual stimulation, inferior culture, irresponsible parents, and so on—which lead to various kinds of unemployabilities, marginal employment, special treatment because of incipient criminality, and so on. The net impact is to detour any real progress and to give a cover of scientific respectability to imposed poverty and enforced unemployment.

Allied to alleged racial inferiority is the attack on possibilities of educational reform. Again, under the mask of liberality, the public school system has been subject to a series of savage attacks. Expert after expert has found reasons to argue that the school lacks the capability to help the poor. Similar to economists who resist formulating noninflationary work strategies, so do the Ivan Illiches, the John Holts, and most

* "The American Resignation: The New Assault on Equality," *Social Policy*, May/June 1972, p. 15.

recently Christopher Jencks refrain from suggesting school programs which could educate people to new and more equitable approaches to work. Jencks concluded that schooling has provided low-income populations almost no greater access to decent income. He argues that more equitable distribution of income is desirable and yet it *never* occurs to him that about the *only* place that discussions about income redistribution could occur is in something like a school. I, years before Christopher Jencks and his colleagues, discovered the limitations of schools, arguing that schools could not change the organization of work when I asserted that "a good education and an imperfect employment system can only lead to many well-educated people being unable to find work."*

And yet at the same time I advocated that schools must be a place where work creation through fiscal, monetary, and public service employment policies be discussed. That aspect of schooling for a desirable work world, "liberals" like Christopher Jencks never even begin to address. Jencks and his colleagues conclude that factors outside school are more important than school in determining work roles, but they never analyze *why* schools play so limited a role or what could conceivably be done in a school designed to make the American Dream a reality.*

While some vision killers are trying to decry the possibilities of full employment, others discuss the implausibility of equal opportunity, others argue for the validity of current admissions standards to work in universities, and yet others "realistically" evaluate the potentiality of schools, yet another fifth column suggests that what *is*—is defensible and just. So it's not surprising to find Nathan Glazer, frequent coauthor with Daniel Patrick Moynihan, arguing that war financing

* Arthur Pearl, *The Atrocity of Education* (New York: Dutton, 1972), p. 82.
* See Christopher Jencks et al., *Inequality, a Reassessment of the Effect of Family Schooling in America* (New York: Basic Books, 1972).

does not jeopardize social programs. The evidence he cites is that monies appropriated for social programs have grown rapidly, while the cost of war also increased.† What is left out of Glazer's thinking is the quality of the service affected by distorted priorities, the climate of a nation when it's at war, the loss of social identity when the war is deemed unjust by large numbers of people, and what *could* be accomplished if the military were not draining off resources. Because Nathan Glazer and his coterie have no visions, they have no criteria to make meaningful judgments.

The failure of organized labor

Transcending ideology and cutting across all segments of political thought are allusions to the vitality of organized labor as a force for shaping or reforming work in the United States. At the present time no such potential exists. The leadership of organized labor is in cahoots with prevailing power structures and sentiments. On most important issues, those who speak for labor

- favor activities detrimental to the environment over work compatible with nature because their strength is in goods-producing industries
- oppose any redefinitions of wages or taxes to narrow the gap between the rich and the poor
- refuse to break down the barriers for minorities, women, and other disadvantaged within their own spheres of influence

Organized labor selfishly guards its own turf, more interested in keeping the dues-paying members content than venturing out into broader social areas, treading carefully so that actions will not offend the prejudices of those currently

† *Saturday Review of the Society,* November 1972.

in the fold, and offering no intellectual leadership in meetings, journals, conventions, or in training of rank-and-file leaders. There are exceptions—public workers' unions, farm workers—and there is even some breath of life to be found in the emerging new leadership in old industrial and craft unions.

New leadership of labor is certainly needed to add muscle and depth to a political movement for work reform and to prevent another round of fooling the people at the polls. But, until such leadership emerges, it is folly to place reliance on labor; it borders on the insane to distort the direction and tone of political programs to seduce the aging, and, if not impotent, certainly sterile old men who sit at the helm of the big unions.

What then do we do?

The course ahead for the country is as obvious as it is difficult. There is no alternative but to educate people to the realities of modern macroeconomics. At every level of encounter the policies which create, shape, and deter work must be analyzed with the emphasis on developing new approaches. The president, in his Manpower Report, calls for new emphasis on career education and indeed there should be, but not with the focus that he intends. The stress should *not* be one preparing the student to *fit* into the existing or projected world (although that should be discussed); the focus should be on orienting students to the politics and economics of work, so that students can be masters of their own fates and captains of their own destinies.

The attainment of such a monumental goal would require every person with educational influence to get with it.

Through pre-service and in-service, teachers should be encouraged to generate an intellectual presence concerning work. They should be able to discuss the implications of state and federal budgets, the workings of the credential society, the impact of various kinds of work on the environment, the "pros" and "cons" of public service employment; also, the logical work consequences of a free economy dictated by the "invisible hand of the market," of a partially controlled economy using government as stabilizer through manipulation of taxes, interest rates, and "employer of last resort," of a totally controlled fascist, socialist, or communist state, or something that transcends any economic structure now known or hypothesized. These discussions cannot begin too early. The hope is that students would be inspired by engagement with the teacher's provocative intellectual excursions into utopian visions which could be translated into lifelong courses of action: workshops, summer institutes, in-service days, and books for teachers ought to stress such teacher development.

The magazines which can exert an influence on teacher thought must be encouraged to be less provincial. *Saturday Review of Education, Harvard Educational Review, Phi Delta Kappa, Teacher Paper, This Magazine Is about Schools*, and other educational journals ought to be urged to debate various educational approaches about work. These debates should be ongoing and continuous rather than one-shot affairs. The esteemed journals which did so much to launch the new "assault on inequality" ought to be as eager to seek out solutions to pressing problems as they were to pronounce the problems insoluble.

The magazines which specifically address work activities— *In the Public Interest*, on the one hand, and *Social Policy*, on the other—representing diverse perspectives, ought to debate issues in their pages rather than fire broadsides at each other. These debates must try to resolve the apparent contradictions between economic growth and environmental stability, propose solutions to poverty and racism, defend the calculations of the costs of different microeconomic policies—military spending, social insurance, subsidies, tax strategies, and so on.

Hopefully, some newspapers would find it in the public interest to feature syndicated columnists analyzing work from diverse perspectives; these columnists would get as much "ink" as those writing about the stock market, bridge, and who was seen with whom at Frank Sinatra's Palm Beach hideaway.

To shock the nation into some consciousness, the exotic media can become involved; a series, some spectaculars, a few movies could get people thinking. A Dick Cavett special on "work blues," a series of debates between advocates of free economy, a completely controlled economy, and a quality life economy, sustained long enough for some conclusion, could be as exciting as educationally valuable. Even a situation comedy series could reflect deeply on essential work problems, rather than the few "slapstick" affairs that have been attempted. Charlie Chaplin's *Modern Times*, almost forty years old now, still remains a more penetrating analysis of work in the United States than any TV series or motion picture I can think of.

And, finally, in 1974 many many political office seekers must be inspired either to generate work strategies or commit themselves to already articulated plans. The emergence of several hundred work-aware candidates for state, local, and national positions would both change the nature of national understanding and also, with their election, change government attitudes toward work.

All of these influences could get people thinking positively and any one of us could, by creating visions, stimulate others to do the same.

I have a vision

I have a vision about a work world. A world in which everyone works who desires work. And where the young phase in and the old phase out. It is a work world which

151

emphasizes human services and deemphasizes the manufacturing of things. It is a work world harmonious with nature, a work world which does not depend on coercing people to buy things they don't need, a work world in which *everyone* has equal access to jobs, a work world which offers choice to the job seeker, a work world which generates services (and goods) at least to the extent of demand to ensure a stable dollar, a work world which reduces the gap between the highest paid full-time worker and the lowest to $6,000 a year, a work world based on the notion that those who have the most pay the most to maintain their government, a work world organized into decentralized, relatively autonomous units to avoid unnecessary bureaucratic inhumanities and facilitate worker and client satisfaction. In my vision it is a work world organized to build livable cities and convenient, comfortable, and ecologically defensible transportation, a work world that addresses hunger, a work world that reduces the need for crime, a work world with more doctors than policemen, a work world that generates three times as much income in education than in finance, insurance, and real estate (the reverse holds true today). My vision of a work world is *economically* feasible, economically desirable, and psychologically gratifying. My work world is also possible *politically*.*

Assume that such a vision was in existence today. What would be its distinguishing feature? How many people would be working? What would they be doing? How would they be prepared for work? What would be the pay scale? Who would pay for such work? What guarantees of satisfaction would there be for worker or persons served?

* What is presented here must be a bare outline of a vision. For a more complete presentation, see Arthur Pearl and Frank Riessman, *New Careers for the Poor* (New York: Free Press, 1965) ; Arthur Pearl, *Atrocity of Education*; and Arthur Pearl, "The Human Service Society—an Ecological Perspective," in Riessman, Nixon and Gartner (ed.) , *Public Service Employment* (New York: Praeger, 1973) .

A full-employment society in 1969 would have created 162 million jobs (more than twice the number actually employed on an average day in that year). The work would be structured so that the very young could phase in and the old could phase out. For every age group, some persons, because of other commitments or interests, would work only part time.

It is well known that young people can perform useful roles in society: eight-year-olds can tutor six-year-olds, five-year-olds can help clean up nursery schools, persons of almost any age can remove litter or plant trees or tend to a vegetable garden. The fact that presently the young are denied opportunities to contribute to a community partially explains the high incidence of alienation reflected in crime and drug abuse among such a population, and this form of alienation cuts deeply into affluent populations almost to the extent that it afflicts the poor.

The following table shows how this could work.

TABLE 9
Hypothesized labor force characteristics in a true full employment society

Age	Population (in millions)	Percent Participation	Labor Force	Percent of Time Employed	Labor Force in Full Time Equivalents
All ages	203.2	79.6	161.8	—	111.2
Under 5	17.2	1	.2	20	.0
5–13	36.6	50	18.3	30	5.4
14–17	15.8	90	15.3	50	7.6
18–24	23.7	99	23.5	70	16.4
25–34	24.9	99	24.7	80	19.8
35–44	23.1	99	22.9	90	20.6
45–54	23.3	98	22.8	90	20.5
55–64	18.6	97	18.1	80	14.5
Over 65	20.0	80	16.0	40	6.4

SOURCE: Generated from U.S. Bureau of Census data, 1964.

To ensure that such an employment system wasn't inflationary, the public would be educated to buy no more than was needed. Television "commercials" would point out the stupidity of buying a new suit when last year's is still serviceable; Joe Namath would be shown wearing last year's suits, driving (and then only rarely) a ten-year-old car and using an even older corn popper (there is no way that electric corn poppers can be as much fun as the old-fashioned kind that used the energy heating the house). Through regulation of taxes and interest rates, aggregate demand would be kept in bounds and, since the educational systems at every level of the society would explain the need for such procedures, these restrictions would be a part of a democratic process rather than a dictatorial imposition (accountability of leadership was discussed in earlier chapters). In much the same way prices would be influenced. The two most important components in determination of the cost of a "thing" or service would be the argument made for provision of quality life and the drain on the environment. For example, a limousine which offers no better transportation than a more modest automobile and uses excessive amounts of metals in its construction and fossil fuel in its operation would cost in the millions of dollars (the additional costs being in the form of taxes that would offset the price of vital health or conservation services).

The wages paid people in a society would also be regulated; a runaway wage structure *must* be earth-depleting. Persons with large amounts of money must spend it; once the basic needs of hunger, shelter, and clothing are met, the money *must* be spent on trinketry or trivia. These forms of affluence, as Philip Slater in *The Pursuit of Loneliness* and Martin Buber in a variety of his writings have shown, lead to curious forms of alienation and breakdown of communities, leaving the beneficiaries bereft of feelings of meaningful existence, competence, belonging, and usefulness. A wage structure falling within the perimeters of 1970 economic activity could have the characteristics shown in the following table:

TABLE 10
Wages in full employment, human service society—1970 U.S. economic activity

Yearly Wage (in dollars)	Number of Workers (in millions)	Total Wages (in billions)
2,000	20	40
3,000	10	30
4,000	10	40
5,000	20	100
6,000	30	180
7,000	20	140
8,000	20	160
9,000	10	90
10,000	10	100
11,000	5	55
12,000	5	60
TOTAL	160 million	995 billion

Median Income $6,667

The lowest wages would be paid those working part time (the very lowest, paid to very young children working a very few hours, is excluded from this table) and the highest wages would be paid to persons in sensitive leadership positions. Before anyone gets alarmed at the proposed depressed wage conditions, bear in mind that $6,667 is three times the *median* wage of all persons receiving wages in the United States in 1970. Keep in mind that, with a full employment economy, more than one person would likely be earning wages in a family and that services would be available at deflated fees and prices. Such a system would preclude the economic obscenities of professional athletes and other entertainers receiving enormous salaries while literally millions are mired

155

in behavioral sinks of ghettos and reservations—and the political distortions that such discrepancies bring.

What would 160 million people be doing? *Some would be building new cities*; five hundred new cities consisting of no more than 250,000 persons could be created in the United States in the next twenty-five years. These cities should be so organized that walking would be a major means of getting to work, to theaters, to schools, to shopping centers, and so on. They would be organized centripetally, they would *not* segregate into neighborhoods of different economic conditions and racial backgrounds.

Some of the 160 million would be working in transportation—convenient mass transit systems *must* be developed to replace a dependency on the privately owned fossil fuel–consuming vehicle. The private automobile depletes the world's oil (increasing the risk of war), polluting the air and waterways. It has to go! Exciting systems can replace it and generate in the process millions of jobs. Some workers would continue to be involved in manufacturing "goods," but the number employed on a full-time basis would be markedly reduced; even in "goods" production there would be encouragement of smaller, more technologically primitive operations, again to conserve energy and materials.

The majority of the people would work in human services: medicine, where practitioners would be doubled; education, which would provide persons in teaching roles for every 10 people in the society (a fivefold increase). Millions of people would be involved repairing, restoring, and extending the livability of the environment; food production in smaller, more diversified, closer-to-home acreage would be encouraged (to replace the support of monoculture, distant, huge agro-industries); again, in this system human activities would be featured over machines and the farm worker would be encouraged to find gratification in his work through provision of health, educational, cultural, housing, and other services. The following table contrasts the distribution of work in existing and in visionary circumstances.

TABLE 11
Distribution of work in the existing goals-oriented society and in the proposed human service society (1970 figures)

	EXISTING Numbers % (in millions)		PROPOSED Numbers % (in millions)		FTE Numbers % (in millions)	
TOTAL WORK FORCE	75.0	100	161.8	100	111.2	100
Mining	.6		.5		.4	
Construction	3.3		4.0		3.0	
Manufacturing	19.4	25.9	16.0	9.4	10.0	9.0
Transportation and Public Utilities	4.5		10.0		6.0	
Wholesale and Retail Trade	15.0		14.0		9.0	
Services (other than Human Services)	8.5		7.0		5.0	
Medical (private)	3.1		5.0		4.0	
Government (including human services)	12.6	20.8	94.3	61.4	63.8	61.0
Agriculture	4.3		9.0		6.0	

SOURCE: Bureau of Labor Statistics.

NOTE: To emphasize differences in work activities, only selected jobs are shown in this chart.

The projected work world would reduce reliance on petroleum considerably and thereby allow others in the world to gain access to quality life. The United States has more than doubled its consumption of oil in the last twenty years. The government has encouraged such profligate use of a depletable resource, Mr. Nixon has been very supportive of the oil industry, and they have reciprocated. Such a policy is not only *not* in the public interest but is actually suicidal and no amount of blustering will alter that reality; only a work world emancipating human dependency from fossil fuels can deflect us from impending doom. This vision does just that.

How would people get ready for work? The credential society—so necessary when there isn't enough work to go around and as a cover for race, class, sex, and ethnic discrimination—requires that persons be warehoused in schools for many years before allowed entrance into the work world. Keeping people in school increases the not-in-the-labor-force numbers, while creating the illusion of low unemployment. Long-term required schooling as prerequisite for work excludes the poor because of the costs and because of covert discrimination. Requiring many years of school before work entrance is *not* in the interests of quality standards. The work world and the school world are remote; activity in one has almost no relevance to the other (the *one* lesson that should have been learned in the sixties). The logical answer is to bring the two closer together. This is not to be accomplished, as Ivan Illich suggests, in a *Deschooling Society*, but rather in a schooling society which both relates to work for periods of time and allows reflection for other periods. One way that the merger of education and work could be accomplished is *New Careers* (elaborated in a book that Frank Riessman and I wrote), which creates entry work positions in all service fields available to all (regardless of previous experience, training, or alleged ability) and allows individuals to augment work experience with formal education after they have begun to work; the access to education and training is available throughout life.

The continued lifelong education, the reduction of reliance on technical structures, the increased availability of work all act as brakes on bureaucratic intransigence. There can be no *assurance* that brutality will not again be imposed on worker and client, but the availability of choice for worker and persons served is the greatest guarantee against such an abuse. The issue of choice to the consumer of service must be addressed. Richard Nixon profited greatly from the dissatisfaction of the service customer; it is this dissatisfaction that he used to justify cutbacks in social programs. The vision shared here does provide choice to the student, patient, client, park-goer, and so on. Only a part of the services will be underwritten by government; the rest will be negotiated by the interested parties. The negotiations will be restricted in the exchange of monies and will be augmented by the availability of service personnel. The single most important need in medicine, for example, is more and different practitioners. The single most important need in education, on the other hand, is choice for students and their parents. The vision allows for both by (1) creating the work, and (2) increasing the consumer's buying power.

Who would pay for all this work? The pay would come from both fees *and* taxes. The tax structure would require heavy taxation of the haves, both to reduce their economic importance and to provide the means for a societal change. If you think that such a tax strategy implies killing the goose laying the polluted eggs—you are correct. Big industry which commits crimes against Nature can be no more encouraged than any other form of organized crime. But discouraging big industry means encouraging other industry. Assuming a $995 billion economy, $660 billion would be reflected in fees and goods exchanges and $330 billion in taxes (which is about what is raised now) ; the difference is that the $660 billion will not enhance private wealth and $330 billion will be used to generate needed services. A president, in my vision, would make no more than $12,000 a year. If he wanted to be a king, he could go somewhere else. The tax structure would guarantee the service, the user fee would give the customer choice, and the regulating process of government would act to maintain balance by buffering inflation and equalizing distribution. The economics is not the question; the issue is the will.

The political potential of any vision is reflected in its first steps toward implementation. The simple most important first step toward my vision is the creation of meaningful, universally available service occupations. To learn the lesson of the sixties is to recognize that organization of work is the key to elimination of poverty, racism, war, and ecological disaster. The work needed is human public service. The first act is a significant Public Service Employment Bill. By 1974 this bill should be providing funds for 10 million persons in health, education, welfare (redefined as helping people cope) , recreation, esthetics, and conservation. The $70 billion (perhaps more because of the inflation Richard Nixon encourages) would come from new priorities, cutbacks in military, subsidies, and tax shelters for the rich. The number of new positions would easily absorb all the persons displaced by the rearrangement in priorities and the transfer would be facilitated by a new career strategy that offered training and education *after* employment.

At the time of writing, a public service bill more modest, but nonetheless significant, is sponsored by Senator Cranston and Congressman Hawkins. This bill or something like it must be supported. *Social Policy*,* a periodical which discusses aspects of public employment, should be read and supported, as should an organization for public service employment.†

* Suite 500, 184 Fifth Ave., New York, N.Y.
† 358 Broadway, New York, N.Y. 10013.

Summary--so there we have it

We have found Richard Nixon in the White House for a second term, getting there by a systematic attack on the integrity of a work world, using his office to increase unemployment, to decrease the buying power of the worker, to impede progress to social equality, to enable the rich to get richer at the expense of everyone else and succeeding because of confusion.

The confusion eroded political thought. Myths were worshiped and knowledge deplored in the left, right, and middle. The scientific disciplines got bogged down in sectarian squabbles. Economists fought over whether full employment was inflationary. Biologists pondered whether livelihood wouldn't destroy livability. Psychologists postulated whether any concern for work didn't reflect repressive early childhood toilet training. No one offered solutions, no one dared to dream.

If you out there, in front of a TV or the sports pages, somehow find it hard to get with all this because it is complicated and no nice neat solutions jump up for you to grab, and, therefore, you're willing to let things deteriorate and are content to let the Richard Nixons of the world do your thinking for you, try to calculate the costs of such laziness. And, after you have added it up, remember one thing: Sucker, you paid.

161

CHAPTER SEVEN

The quality of life is strained
   OR,
There is more to life than
work and war

More and more, American life becomes counterfeit. A counterfeit people have no choice but to elect a counterfeit president. That is the message of election 1972. The election of
the president signified that a nation had lost its authenticity.
True political change will be signaled by a return to authenticity. Authenticity is not synonymous with decency, justice,
freedom or equality. It merely addresses the sham, strips off
the gleaming veneer of technical progress, and sheds light on
the mess that stinks and stagnates underneath. The muckrakers of the past did that—they told the truth about America—
it wasn't a truth easy to accept and those who could hear no
evil didn't accept it. But the truth they told *was* reflected at
the polls and in the market place of ideas. The truth they
told wasn't kind, but it permitted a genuine pride and fostered national purposes. The telling of truth defines social
space; it tells us who we are. The "who we are" may be nei-

ther noble nor fair, but in this truth is the legitimate comfort of recognition. The reality of our existence, ignoble and even base, because it is understandable, can be tolerated and even enjoyed. Pain is far more desirable than no feeling at all. A real people can laugh and love. Such reality has warmth, tenderness, and hurt. A real people harbor their dreamers, are open about their bigotry, their jingoism, their selfishness. A real people accept leaders for what they are and more important, accept the responsibility for *putting* leaders *where* they are. We are losing all of that. It gets harder to laugh all the time or to define ourselves other than in the things we own. Parents are shocked to discover that their own children are really strangers. School administrators are horrified if any teacher acts outside of a carefully prescribed role—and administrators don't have to be horrified often. Wives can't communicate with husbands. Everything about the United States has taken on an unreal eeriness.

Given that this is a reasonably good description, it is certainly logical that the most unreal among us should be our president.

The United States is counterfeit because it has lost its soul. Soul, as blacks use the term, to describe a basic bond between people sharing a common destiny; but also soul as a manifestation of an ambition that transcends day-to-day material indecencies. Mephistopheles came in the form of a computer, a garbage disposal, an eight-cylinder souped-up LTD, a house in the suburbs, and we *gave* ourselves to him. We didn't even bargain. We never asked the price and, when he came to take us away, we never even protested. It was so subtle that we never knew it happened.

When last checked, stocks in soul had plummeted on the Dow-Jones averages almost to the extent that industrials were up.

The quality of life—the feelings of security, comfort,

belonging, usefulness, meaning, and competence that we aim for in every arena of our existence—work, politics, culture, leisure, and personal encounters—has slipped through grasping fingers. No one ever really described the Midas malady. It has a curious syndrome—the gold comes off on the fingers which causes the joints to stiffen, thereby precluding the grasping of significance. Having goldfingers is a far more serious ailment than having butterfingers. And yet no one with goldfingers ever gets booed.

What Goldwater couldn't do in 1964, Goldfinger did in 1972.

In the equation Quality of Life = Security + Comfort + Competence + Usefulness + Meaning + Belonging, the last three variables comprise soul. The United States—as a people in a mad rush for security, obscene comfort, and individual competence—chose quantity over quality and when you choose quantity—you can never get enough.

The counterfeiting of a nation, the losing of authenticity, doesn't happen all at once. It is *not* a now-you-have-it-now-you-don't proposition. It is never totally there or totally lost. The erosion is slow and imperceptible.

The United States lost its soul as humans gave way to machines in economic activity.

The United States lost its soul as health, education, and other human services grew and were governed by tables of organization and manuals of operation.

The United States lost its soul as culture was packaged to elucidate nothing and as films and novels disguised heroes and heroines with pasted-on nakedness.

The United States lost its soul on a freeway somewhere between the centrifugalized suburbs and the centripetalized ghettos.

The United States lost its soul as humans passed their corruption on to Nature.

The United States lost its soul in indifference to poverty and class and race justice—the soul that couldn't be bottled up in prisons was bottled up in country clubs.

The United States lost its soul as the sum total of its mentality was found on bumper strips and as its ideology degenerated into graffiti.

Persons without soul welcome a presidential invitation to do things for themselves because they *know* that translates into asking, What can *I take* for myself?

People without soul proudly proclaim an indifference to their brother's misfortune, forgetting that he whom they plagiarize was his brother's murderer.

Persons without soul desperately grope inward, clumsily tearing at their innards, to discover themselves. As they play at sensitivity, they sacrifice their intelligence upon an altar of counterfeit feelings.

Persons without soul rise as sheep to ask in rhetorical song whether the United States remains a land of the free and home of the brave while both attributes continue to decline; and pledge allegiance to freedom and justice for all only to sneer savagely at those who have neither.

A nation without soul—steals! Property crime in the United States goes up. In 1969 more than one out of 50 people had property stolen; that was twice the rate of 1960. The United States has become a "rip-off" society. A modern Descartes might philosophize, "I rip-off, therefore I am!" Stealing isn't the exclusive province of the underclass, the ungrateful wretches that progress left behind. Stealing is everybody's pastime. The middle income do it, only they call in tax experts to assist them. The super rich do it; that's how they acquired their wealth. The super rich needn't worry. They will not be brought before the bar of justice. They protected themselves—they stole the government. They are generous and reward loyal servants. Thus we find people with little personal means become congressmen, work at modest salaries, serve a few terms, and retire—rich! What was it Mark Twain said? Oh, yes, "It could probably be shown by facts and figures that there is no distinctly American criminal class except Congress." And Twain said that way back when he and others were doing everything possible to define and defend an authentic America. There is some small sobering solace to discover that Richard Nixon is reducing Congress to a *petty* criminal status. A nation devoid of soul isn't a whit interested in whether its president is involved in hanky-panky at the Watergate apartments or if his campaign fund raising is illegal.

A nation without soul—cannot tolerate truth. Sometimes truth is avoided by outright lies. The lies come from everywhere but no record is kept so no statistics can be quoted, but undoubtedly lies have grown at least at the rate that stealing has increased. Lies come from the top. Thus one president lies (or is lied to) about how we got into a war, another president lies (or is lied to) about how we got out. The second president tells newsmen that *they* "gag" when *he* talks about honorable peace, not aware that *that* lie ought to stick in *his* throat. Sometimes lies come from the bottom; these are the lies that Rollo May calls pseudo-innocence. Voters lie when they accuse McGovern of fuzziness, thus disguising their own indolence and incompleteness—sure McGovern could be clearer, but the real culprit was the voter who proclaimed a competence that he or she never had. Still others play the evasion game to prop up a society likely to fall apart from its inauthenticity. Here we find the mythmakers, the idols of idiot worshippers sanctified by ordination at Delphian universities. We find a war on poverty launched on a lie—the alleged inferiority of the poor—rather than on the *real* inequities of power and pelf in societal institutions. Lies are told by persons who clearly stand to profit from their lies and their conflict of interest isn't challenged. Lies are told by neutralists who claim authenticity because of their disengagement, as if truth is *ever* midway between extremes. Thus by speaking with forked tongues on both sides of a controversy they offer nothing of use to either. Lies come screaming from persons behind lecterns or are seductively transmitted in staged encounters where cowards take cheap shots by telling others "how they come across"; lies come back many times transmogrified and adroitly programmed on television. In a soulless society (to paraphrase Yeats), How *can* you know the liar from the lie?

A nation without soul—maims and murders. Crimes against people markedly increased in the United States. In 1960, 27,605 persons were known victims of homicide or suicide; by 1967 the number had risen to 34,720, an increase of 26 per cent in just seven years—far greater than the increase in population. Crimes of violence increase but also become more senseless—movie pople get mutilated, farm laborers are murdered en masse, women in Boston are strangled. All these deaths became strangely legitimate in an illegitimate society.

A soulless society turns to drugs. The desperation that comes with an ungenuine existence is countered with psychoactive chemistry. The *rate* of drug arrests increased from 31 per 100,000 people in 1960 to 183 per 100,000 people in 1969—that's a sixfold increase! The relation between a Richard Nixon reelection and a drug-indulging society is not simple but it is fathomable. The drugs are merely a symptom of mindlessness, of simple inadequate adjustments to a complex society. It is not necessarily true that dopers voted for Richard Nixon, but the people who voted for him were doing what drug users do; they were unwilling to check out the validity of their own behavior. Richard Nixon was to the 60 percent who swept him into office what heroin is to an addict. And the analogy holds because, once *in*, both agents, through increased dependency, erode even further an authentic life.

A soulless people are selfish. They find reasons to be unempathetic. They *fought* against spending money to reduce poverty but they *bought* the argument of poor people's deficits and objected to paying for such unworthies. Selfishness maintains racism, selfishness justifies misuse of earth, selfishness leads to war, selfishness means that many pets eat better than billions of people, selfishness is "I've got mine, you have yours to get." Selfishness means hounding welfare recipients and cutting back on financial assistance to poor college students, selfishness means outlandishly high salaries for professional athletes and medical doctors and outrageously low income for people who work on farms—a selfishness that is short-sighted, self-destructive, weird.

The responses to crime and drugs reflect counterfeit existence. Crime is countered by repressive laws and more police, which do not help the problem but do get in the way of due process and other basic rights. The intertwining of crime and the inauthenticity of technical being can only be effectively dealt with at root cause. Drug abuse *will not* be ameliorated by professional football stars making TV commercials in which they say that they don't use drugs so we shouldn't either—which is close to explaining why indeed drugs are used. Drug abuse will be countered when opportunities are created so that people can obtain fulfillment without the need for chemically inspired stimulants, depressants, or hallucinogens. That society would offer legitimate *choice* in work, political matters, culture, leisure, and personal growth to everyone. That society would be redemptive and allow persons once involved in drugs to reenter a functioning society without the heavy weight of stigma. That society *could not* be handed out on a platter because no one owns it

169

to give away, although those with wealth and power in public government and private industry are able to do more to increase options than those without influence in either. A good society would in fact point to its flaws and invite everyone to participate in building a better work world, a more complete democracy, a greater cultural diversity, and so on. That society would be a hand up to those who have fallen, a beacon to those who have lost their way. The stupidity of terrorizing persons out of drugs by threat of police action is exceeded only by teasing them out of addiction with TV commercials, and yet both treatments seem innocuous when compared to that huge gargoyle perched on the neck of a totally beaten human being and all the while it is exercising excruciating pressure it leans forward to mock—"Ask only what you can do for yourself."

An inauthentic society does funny things to people. Traditional liberals became reactionary. Jews caught in conflict over international squabbles, affirmative action in employment, crime, and housing in the inner city turned toward Richard Nixon. In one sense this *is* surprising: Nixon, as California politician, was despised by most Jewish voters. His campaign against Helen Gahagan Douglas left deep and bitter wounds for most Jews who saw in this campaign the brand of tactics that not so distantly had led Hitler to power in Germany. But the absence of soul bit deeply into modern Jewry. Jewish intellectuals found themselves attacked by nonwhite minorities. Jewish shopkeepers in the ghetto were sacked, Jewish Ph.D.s were bypassed for *some* university appointments in favor of nonwhites; Jewish Zionists were terrified that little Israel would be betrayed in the cynical give-and-take of the Big Powers. So Jews, once America's foremost radicals, finding themselves displaced and not liking the language, tone, and manners of the new leftists, succumbed to the blandishments of inauthenticity and found that Richard

Nixon became more and more acceptable. Almost half the Jews were in some way the central figure of Huxley's *After Many a Summer Dies the Swan* who, adjusting to the three hundred-year-old decomposing horror of degenerated humanity, observed that "he wasn't too bad when you get used to him"—and so too did many Jews find that Richard Nixon wasn't too bad when you got used to him.

Even the 11 percent of the blacks who voted for Richard Nixon (and the much larger number who never even bothered to vote) got entangled in the inauthenticity of their world. The blacks, in their efforts to establish community in a technological society which denies community, are, like all tormented populations, torn by dissension. Rich blacks, beneficiaries of black capitalism, found class more important than race. Other blacks, precisely because of their underclass position and declining prospects, and even though the world was surrendering any commitment to decency, could not renounce hope (extremely affluent populations can afford the luxury of pessimism, which may explain *their* high suicide rates). Hope takes many forms. For some, it is the belief that the system *is* open and that they too can make it big in a free enterprise economy, voting for Richard Nixon as *the* symbol of free enterprise in a declaration of hope. Another factor could be fear—vulnerable populations must be suspicious—and a percentage reasoned that a vote against Nixon was a declaration of war, one that they were hardly in a position to fight. And some found gratification in picking a winner. Voting can be somewhat like playing the numbers or the ponies—the payoff, while not monetary, could be psychologically gratifying. And yet, for all the explaining, the key fact remained—*very few blacks voted for Richard Nixon*—and, since the thesis is that those who did were fooled, where does that put people who insist that the *least* foolish among us— are intellectually inferior?

171

Other minorities were attracted to Richard Nixon because of the basic flaws in the poverty programs. Richard Nixon "seized the time" in exploiting the intergroup conflict over poverty program funds. In the beginning of the poverty program, way back in 1965, the chief beneficiaries were blacks. They, because of inner-city location and incipient organization, were able to muster a sufficient squeak to get some grease. Other minority groups, particularly Native Americans and Mexican-Americans (Chicanos), followed shortly, but found that when they got there the grease gun was dry!—ah, Mother Hubbard, where *are* you when we need you? The net result was bitter warring over what was much too little for any one group. Nixon, recognizing that he had very few black votes, shifted poverty support to the next largest group—the Spanish-speaking minorities. He placed a California Mexican-American (an unsuccessful Republican political aspirant) at the head of the Office of Economic Opportunity. He placed in desks throughout that and other agencies with related concerns brown-skinned persons where previously blacks sat. The pitting of one underclass against another helps build inauthenticity in the United States.

The loss of authenticity made Richard Nixon readily acceptable to the bigot. He mopped up there; he was perceived (in the absence of George Wallace) as the last white hope against a rising tide of enforced integration. He was an ally in the campaign against bussing which was so popular a cause he didn't even get in trouble with the Greyhound people. He was "our" man because he wasn't going to allow those blankety-blank nonwhites to walk all over those of us who made this country what it is today. Richard Nixon gained votes because of his resolute stand against welfare chiselers (who were, in bigots' eyes, "blacks"). He made a killing with his stand on law and order; here the average, ordinary, hail-fellow-well-met bigot *knew* he was talking about *nonwhite*-inspired crime in the streets. The talk about law and order produced no law and no order but the bigot wasn't prepared for anything more than talk—anything more and he, the bigot, would have to change—so Mr. Nixon came to them as ghost of elections past and said vote for me and you need not change, I will make the world into what it was—and that was comfort, and that was security, and that allowed a sense of competence—and that was the bite in the neck that fattens vampires.

The blue-collar worker, the heart of the alliance that was once the Democratic party, was in election 1972 introduced to the tip of the iceberg of selfishness and recoiled much like a terrified soldier fingering the edges of a gaping wound. There can be, for the blue-collar worker, the Jew, the academic intellectual, women, and the young, no true new alliance, no new political breakthrough—nothing, without some form of thaw, a warmth that comes with new ideas—otherwise, the Richard Nixons will be candidates for both parties and Will Rogers would, if he was alive, have to amend his comment that he never met a man he didn't like to include robots.

How would we recognize a quality life if we were introduced to it?

A quality life is choice in everything we do. A quality life is a measure of control over our physical and social environments. A quality life means an opportunity to choose the nature of work and to change when that choice is no longer attractive.

A quality life is political power, not only at the presidential level where we, the average voters, have been taken for granted—the president claims to know what we believe but he never asks our advice—the choice must also be at state and local governments. And yet politics extends beyond government, politics includes everywhere, and we must have power in nongovernmental politics, in ecological self-help activities, in neighborhood associations, in bowling leagues, and so on. Here, too, must there be opportunity to sense security, comfort, competences *and* belonging, usefulness and meaning.

A quality life is understanding that government is really in the business of raising and spending money; if the money is raised unfairly or spent unwisely, the average citizen's quality of life is diminished.

A quality life is a life of quality service. Everyone must be allowed the feeling of being a valued human when sick in the hospital, when searching for work at an employment center, when stopped by a policeman for exceeding police laws, when applying for admission to a university, when requesting a driver's license, a business license, a dog license.

If there are said to be over a half-million policemen in the United States, how come they are so rarely around when the average citizen needs them? Why aren't policemen available to escort women home to *prevent* assault, rape, and murder?

Why aren't mental health practitioners available to stay the night in the homes of persons who need support and reassurance during trying times?

Why isn't there a round-the-clock adequately staffed day care center, and a doctor on call, in every national park?

Why aren't there helpers available to assist the aged in every facet of their lives?

A quality life is reflected in culture. Why isn't everyone, at every age, provided the opportunity to participate in the arts? Why aren't there artists in residence in every neighborhood? Do you think that a Jimi Hendrix would be dead today if there was some solid support for his musical contributions? If he had opportunity to teach? to grow? to experiment? If he wasn't a captive of the fans who adored him?

Why isn't there a *place* for adolescents to go to legitimately escape adults?

A quality life is reflected in the humanization of institutions—schools, retirement services, and prisons which encourage human growth. A quality life is one in which each of us is more than an account in some massive computerized data bank.

A quality life is asking and answering new questions. A quality life is an education for personal and social responsibility, which brings me back to the vision killers.

Vision killers and quality life, starring the Dead End Kids from Harvard

Throughout this book I have, while rushing at full speed, lashed out at various people, mostly social scientists, calling them "vision killers." The attack, until now, has been more rhetorical than substantial and thus no more defensible than *their* set of behaviors. At this point, I would like to slow down and offer a more thorough presentation because nothing is more crucial to a quality life than an understanding of the social processes which create or impede such development. The role that social scientists have played in the "retreat from education" is representative of academic irresponsibility and hence provides an excellent example for a more complete study.

Philosophers in almost every historical era have fretted about educated man's capacity to emancipate himself from his miseries. In the 1920s and 1930s in the United States some pioneering efforts were made, by John Dewey in particular, to translate ethical postulates into practical action. The actions were tentative, controversial, and inconclusive.

At the beginning of the sixties, after a gap of over twenty years (apart from some foot-dragging following the unanimous 1954 Supreme Court decision ordering desegregation of schools), the question of the school's relation to social equality was raised again. The central thesis concerned the failure of nonwhite minorities, particularly black Americans, to achieve economic equality in these United States. James B. Conant of Harvard and elsewhere sounded the alarm in *Slums and Suburbs** that "social dynamite was building up in the slums" in the form of large numbers of Negro (the term well-mannered educated people used in those days) dropouts. This report, and others not as widely heralded, provoked a rash of experiments. Within the schools, antidropout campaigns were begun. James Brown assisted by singing, "Don't be a fool, stay in school"—and other activities of similar depth were attempted. For those who had already dropped out, work training and counseling programs were initiated primarily under the sponsorship of the U.S. Labor Department to whom or to which Harvard released Daniel Patrick Moynihan to serve as special assistant to the secretary.

From such modest beginnings came the much advertised social programs of the Kennedy-Johnson administrations and the later pronouncements of failure that so greatly assisted the political career of Richard Nixon.

The assumptions which undergirded the New Frontier and Great Society programs, as enunciated by a group of social scientists suddenly skyrocketed from youthful obscurity into the spotlight of national importance, were the following:

1. Economic success was predicated on school success. Therefore, the longer one went to school, the better would be the quality of life.

2. Black (and other poor) students were unable to complete school because of a number of serious defects. At this point, the new social planners branched out into three schools:

In School A were found personality-oriented psychologists

* James B. Conant, *Slums and Suburbs* (New York: McGraw-Hill, 1961).

who argued that chaotic home conditions and the existence of an extended family seriously disrupted the social growth of the student and that student, because he demanded instant gratification and was otherwise unable to control his impulses, could not be expected to succeed in school.

In School B were found learning-oriented psychologists and sociologists taken with linguistics, who argued that the lack of books or other printed material in the home and illiterate parents with restricted languages and life styles depreciating intellectual activities lead to school failure stemming from accumulated environmental deficit.

In School C were found sociologists and anthropologists who argued that the blacks and other generational poor had developed a well-entrenched "culture of poverty" with highly institutionalized antiintellectual values, mores, and norms which precluded school success.

3. Equality of opportunity could be achieved by, rather simply and inexpensively, overcoming the deficits of the poor:

Those in School A advocated that the poor be provided highly structured consistent environments which socialized them to fit into the school environment and enabled them to grow from "pleasure principle" orientation to a reality orientation based on delayed gratifications. Translated into proposals and budgets, this approach called for lots of special counseling, work training programs, such as the Job Corps, and special classes in elementary and high schools.

Those in School B opted for head starts and other remedial language programs. Such programs, based on assumptions of limited skill, meant that the students were subjected to dreary drills to train them to speak, read, spell, and write *the* language of the American people.

Those in School C divided into one group who didn't want to do anything—they loved *studying* the poor and hoped to see them remain as kind of living museums—while another group suggested instituting something like religious proselytization of heathens. This latter approach meant that blacks and other minorities had to abandon their historical roots as excess baggage for the train ride to future success.

Programs based on all three schools of thought were attempted. In a very few years the youthful protagonists aged and, as failure followed failure, the glow and thrill dissipated into cynicism and despair. Having failed the poor, the social scientists lashed out at those *they* had let down.

And very suddenly old pessimisms replaced impetuous optimisms. The thesis *had* looked like this:

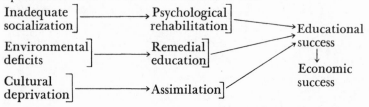

Because of inadequate response, this theory *had* to be revised.

And in the revision two old chestnuts were dusted off and reannounced as *scientific* breakthroughs.

One theme stressed the genetic inferiority of the poor, particularly the nonwhites. The other decreed that schools were insignificant social institutions. If either view is accepted, the formula for economic success breaks down. If the genetic inferiority theory holds, academic success becomes impossible and thus the path to *economic success* is no longer accessible. If the thesis that schools are marginal is accepted, educational success is unrelated to economic success. Both of these views were presented as dangerous myths in the last chapter; they are now reexamined in the context of their claim to scientific importance.

The thesis of racial genetic inferiority is deeply embedded in American intellectual thought. Thomas Jefferson was quite specific in his insistence that blacks were inferior to

178

whites in his *Notes on Virginia,* writing long before the Revolutionary War, although he didn't have the facts to prove it. Anthropology grew as a science in its efforts to classify racial groups. In those classifications, "Negroid" races were defined as clearly inferior on the basis that their alleged sloping foreheads and weak jaws made them more apelike than Caucasians and other superior stocks. The psychologists put the finishing touches on this argument—they created tests which purported to measure innate learning capacity— and on the bases of these tests blacks and other nonwhites were decreed intellectually inferior. This conclusion surfaced during World War I on the basis of performances on the Army Alpha tests when the most renowned psychologists of the time examined the data and concluded that blacks and other nonwhites were inferior races. Almost all of these psychologists, upon reflection, later recanted. And so the matter was dropped for almost twenty years when it was stridently reintroduced by Henry Garrett, president of the American Psychological Association in 1946 and his students. To this day, this group has not wavered in its conclusions, and in fact prompted an official examination by a committee manned by highly regarded leaders of each of the social sciences. Not only was Garrett repudiated in the report of his committee, but the notion of genetic superiority was rejected as being without scientific merit.

Another twenty years elapse; enter now Arthur Jensen. Arthur Jensen hit the big time; newspapers, nationwide, presented abbreviated versions of his articles published in the *Harvard Education Review* and elsewhere; that Arthur Jensen made a wave, stirred a leaf, or even stifled a yawn is remarkable since he offered, by his own admission, no new data. He did even less than that; he treated the *history* of psychology and genetic differences superficially. Thus he left the impression that discounting of social intellectual superiority

179

was a political or moral conclusion symbolic of bleeding-heart liberal mindlessness and not a scientific decision. In one sense Arthur Jensen is right: any decision or even hypothesis about possible racial differences in intelligence transcends science; those kinds of differences could not now (or possibly ever) be detected by scientific procedures.

For genetic-caused racial inferiority to be proved, there must first be developed criteria equally valid for all groups (no such criteria currently exists and it is dubious if such will ever be invented) and, second, each racial group must have equal contact with *desirable* AND *nondesirable* environments. Thus, if one was to *seriously* test for white-black *genetic* differences, white and black children at *conception* would be randomly assigned to different environments, with some black children by chance given prenatal care and childhood supports that the most favored whites now receive; conversely, some white children would grow up like blacks (to reduce observational bias, the children would be appropriately painted so no one but the experimenters—half white and the other half black—would know which was which). Such an experiment is neither feasible nor desirable but *anything* short of that has nothing to do with science. Whenever a person holds to views that are not subject to test, these are not scientific statements but declarations of faith. Mr. Jensen has a right to his religious beliefs but to call them scientific is unwarranted and dangerous.

Now to the group which has dismissed the *possibility* of change through schools. It is certainly as well regarded as the "scientists" who suggest genetic differences and they have much more current data to draw from. In fact, Christopher Jencks' book *Inequality* is literally loaded with figures, as was the celebrated report of James Coleman. The critics of schools have lots of facts—their problem is that the facts they have are irrelevant to the question "What *can* schools do?"

All the *facts* demonstrate that schools *"as currently consti-tuted"* have little impact on economic success. This comes as no surprise to those of us who argued at the very beginning that school programs which tried to rehabilitate the "inade-quately socialized," remediate the "environmentally deficited," and assimilate the "culturally inferior" were doomed because such programs were founded on faulty assumptions. We argued that if there was to be a change in quality life, the *schools* must change in two very clearly defined ways: (1) they must expunge from its processes and purposes all vestiges of institutional racisms, AND (2) they must relate educational offerings to real life challenges.

Institutional racisms will be eliminated: (1) when the race, class, and sex membership of teachers *and administra-tors* is representative of the diverse groups that make up a pluralistic society; (2) when teachers offer equal encourage-ment to all students; (3) when curriculum reflects and respects all underclass life activity, particularly languages and interpretations of history; (4) when extracurricular activities are equitably distributed among all racial classes; and (5) when school governance is revised to guarantee powerless stu-dents the rights of expression, privacy, and due process. For all of these I and others have offered specific proposals—new careers, in-service and pre-service training for teachers, curric-ular outlines, student bills of rights—which have demon-strated on strict scientific grounds considerable promise, and yet the celebrated critics have not seen fit to comment either on the potential for change based on the evidence available, nor have they *analyzed* the resistance of school personnel to change with *any* possibility of change in mind.

The possibility of relevant schools has also been raised. In my book *The Atrocity of Education*, I offer concrete propos-als for changes in schools with respect to work, politics, cul-ture, leisure, and personal growth. Modest experimentation in these areas is sufficiently promising to suggest further work but here again the vision killers are strangely mute.

Instead of looking at schools in terms of some quality life goal, the vision killers lose all direction and thus their comments become aimless mutterings.

An Ivan Illich suggests that societies be deschooled and children be encouraged to learn in networks established primarily in other more economically significant institutions—thus he would turn all education over to those who own the industries, the television networks, the military, or the government.*

What kind of quality life would that complex of leaders suggest for us, and how much tolerance would *they* have for programs that would free souls and break chains (Mark Twain)?

A John Holt subscribes to much the same view; he suggests that children ought to be free to search out their own learning and thus he encourages selfishness—an education without pain, pandering to existing security and the already established competences of a child. That education could be best entitled "Education for Inauthenticity."†

A Neil Postman is even more vague but far more poetic when he suggests that communication is impossible between humans, that media not messages are important, and that children ought to frame their own questions—which means that each one of our selfish existences is equally valid.‡

A. B. F. Skinner suggests that schools be places where children are manipulated like pigeons learning to push levers for food. Implied is that the teachers *own* all the important knowledge and that through consistency of rewards (and punishments) she or he can get children to do what adults

* Ivan Illich, *Deschooling Society* (New York: Harper & Row, 1971).
† John Holt, *How Children Fail* (New York: Dell, 1970).
‡ Neil Postman and Charles Weingartner, *Teaching as a Subversive Activity* (New York: Dell, 1971).

think best—go to war, accept poverty, racism, and so on. Activities based on Skinnerian principles are called Performance Based Contracts and literally millions of dollars are expended trying to get children (mostly poor and nonwhite children) to behave but never to think.§

A Christopher Jencks and his coworkers suggest, in a book heralded as "significant" and "important," that we need socialism in the United States and decides that the way to get it is to renounce school reform as an effective agent for societal change—particularly as an influence to reduce economic inequality:

> There seem to be three reasons why school reform cannot make adults more equal. First, children seem to be far more influenced by what happens at home than by what happens in schools. They may also be more influenced by what happens on the streets and by what they see on television. Second, reformers have very little control over those aspects of school life that affect children. Reallocating resources, reassigning pupils and rewriting the curriculum seldom change the way teachers and students actually treat each other minute by minute. Third, even when a school exerts an unusual influence on children, the resulting changes are not likely to persist into adulthood.*

Thus Jencks argues that schools should not be concerned with long-term effects on "alumni" but, rather, on how much teachers and students enjoy the experience.

None of these statements, and the thousands like them, qualify as scientific statements! They are merely statements of bankruptcy and should be filed as such. The vision killers, having no visions of their own, announce that none are possible. It is nonsensical to expect that schools could produce

§ B. F. Skinner, *Beyond Freedom and Dignity* (New York: Knopf, 1971).
* Christopher Jencks et al., *Inequality: A Reassessment of the Effect of Family and Schooling in America* (New York: Basic Books, 1972), pp. 255–256.

equality—that every person or every group would emerge from a schooling process with equal employment opportunities—it is dubious that such a goal is desirable, let alone possible. That can't happen in school, so why bother to riddle such a straw man? The only effect of such irresponsible attacks is to deflect attention away from real and possible change—the possibility that school could be a place where real problems are discussed and solutions sought. Thus a school would not merely prepare students for a work world, but would be a place where alternative work worlds are debated. It would be a place where a $250 billion budget would be discussed and plans for its spending developed. It would be a place where tax strategies would be analyzed, where model cities and model transportation systems would be constructed, where literature would be produced and art fostered. It would be a place for theater and music.

The school could also be a place where all the community discusses democracy. The school and its relationship to student rights could define and refine civil liberties in new contexts and experiment with different forms of participatory decision making.

The school could be a place where strategies for living compatibly with nature could be devised and at least the possibilities of reducing expenditure of energy resources considered with as much serious intent as proposals for developing new energy resources. Thus poverty and racism could be described, analyzed, and solutions prescribed.

In one sense the school is a marginal institution which explains why bullies delight in kicking it—these are usually people who don't teach and thus argue that no one can. But in another and far more profound sense, the school is central —children do spend a fifth of their lives there—it could be a place where significant problems are attacked significantly. Other institutions—private, industrial, and monetary firms, the military, and the government—do extend more power over us, but these are the institutions most totally captured by inauthenticity. The school by its marginality is most removed from total control. It is one place where a true search can begin and that process can indirectly influence voter mentality which can be reflected in political change which can then alter the impact that powerful corporations and the military exert over our lives.

Christopher Jencks wants socialism. He was able to write a book from the protected environment of a school (Harvard) to call for such a change. Could he have called for socialism as an employee of the Pentagon, of the executive department of the federal government, or of the research staff of General Motors? I think not. An examination of inequality by students in high schools across the country would likely produce at least as defensible a set of conclusions as the Harvard-based team and one far more likely to become a reality.

Schools will become a force for authenticity, however, only when teachers, parents, children, and concerned others get with discussions of appropriate goals at a community level. Such discussions in themselves develop feelings of meaning and belonging. In the last chapter, medicine was described as flawed because of an imbalance between need and supply of service. Education is splattered because of lack of direction. Education directed toward goals could be a crack in bureaucratic totalitarianism. Community discussion is a necessary first step to positive community influence on the schooling process.

At no point do the vision-killing scientists talk about what *could* be. Those of us, as qualified as they (by *their* criteria), who do talk about change and offer concrete proposals, when not ignored by the vision killers are humored at times, and when we get too close to the bone we are ridiculed and dismissed. And yet *we* are close to the data and *we* do the experimenting.

The vision killers are *not* scientists because they are

unwilling to debate or even consider contrary opinions or data. They are not scientists because they will not consider the consequences of their "scientistic" behavior—they have justified every outrageous act on the basis of academic freedom, and if it turned out that their "findings" were used to further the status of the rich and sacrifice the poor *that* was outside their responsibility. Assume that schools were indeed weakened and lost the little educational vitality they have now; the natural consequence would be an even more politically illiterate population than the one we have now. Who then would make the decisions for us—the vision killers? The vision killers do not qualify as scientists because of their remoteness from the people and the institutions they study. They are remote phenomenologically, speaking different tongues and fostering different aspirations, but they are also remote geographically. They study schools and poor people through telescopes but, unlike astronomers who struggle to come closer to the stars, the vision-killing "social scientist" is quite content to keep his distance. But I guess they fail to qualify as scientists mostly because of their arrogance: they are somehow above accountability to anyone; they certainly owe nothing to the poor or to a broader society.

Thus, because of arrogance, insulation, unaccountability, they become—not scientists, but popes. Their pronouncements are not scientific findings but papal bulls. They come not out of careful scrutiny of carefully obtained data but are manifestations of bull-leavings.

The undermining of the belief that schools could be reformed is coupled with similar defeatist statements by "experts" in other fields. All of these are statements which make the baseness of a Richard Nixon acceptable. It is these statements presented as *truth* which leads to the politics of resignation that I mentioned in the earlier chapters.

How, specifically, do we get back our authenticity?

Faust got back his soul by renouncing the selfishness that motivated his original pact with the devil—we could begin with that. We could reject a slogan "Ask what you can do for your country" as a disguised call to war, which indeed it became; we could reject a slogan "Ask what you can do for yourselves" as an open invitation to greed, which indeed it is. Instead, much more humbly, we could "ask what we can do *with* others." Soul implies community: a community at work, a community trying to define and work out problems (that's what politics should mean), a community involved in aesthetics, a community trying to reduce stealing, violence, and drug abuse, a community rearranging living arrangements not dictated by the selfishness of land developers, a community transporting itself no longer at the mercy of General Motors.

A nation regains its authenticity if it struggles for peace (see Chapter 5) and full employment (Chapter 6); that's what Dwight Eisenhower must have been referring to in his farewell address when he warned about a growing military-industrial complex. He must have feared the possibility of war and the destruction of work that came from the three insurgent generals—General Motors, General Foods, and General Westmoreland.

A authentic existence is an enlightened existence. This means that one specific form of change must be in *schooling*. It is perfectly possible in existing schools to inspire children, teachers, and parents to formulate dreams about quality life, develop models for such a life, and even take the first steps.

In schools, children and adults could plan a health service, a police service, a recreational service; they could work out designs for cities for transportation. They could develop land-use regulations. They could define new roles for their elected officials. They could work out mechanisms for more wholesome relationships between races, sexes, and classes. They could phrase questions for their president, such as "If we have to do everything for ourselves, who needs you?"

The questioning of a society and planning for the future is obviously not restricted to the schools; the same question can be phrased anywhere. Newspaper and magazine editors might decide that for balance future plans might be used to counter a steady diet of criticism without prescription.

Politics itself could be a redemptive force. The road back to authenticity begins with reaching out—such reaching out can be furthered as part of political activity. The regaining of soul can be accomplished in the political process of public education, in selection and election of candidates, in maintaining contact with those in power, and, at times, in standing up alone because of the dictates of conscience.

The financing of elections must be altered if there is to be authenticity in our society. A campaign run *by* Big Money must also be a campaign run *for* Big Money. That leaves us no alternative but to think small—to spend no more money than needed, to build a mass base of large numbers of persons contributing modest amounts. The logic presented in Chapter 5 on financing a peace movement can be extended to any political endeavor. My own experience as gubernatorial candidate convinced me that sufficient money can be raised by restricting donations to small amounts; no one could contribute more than $25 to my campaign and, while I didn't win, money was not a significant factor in my loss. In fact, the kind of fun generated by the fund raising—rock festivals, art shows, exotic breakfasts, all kinds of different parties, Christmas card sales (many were artistic successes as much as financial flops)—provided opportunities for contribution that made politics open to persons who had felt excluded, in the process adding authenticity to a life that until then had none. Imagination in fund raising is part of the revitalization of America and there is no escape from educating a people to the *fact* that, if there is to be a quality life for everyone in the United States, *everyone* must pay for a piece of it. A variant of income without work is found in politics without charge and both are equally destructive.

In politics, as elsewhere, if contribution is monopolized by the few, the quality of life must suffer for the majority. In politics and in all other life arenas, each of us should function in such a way that it is possible for every other person to be a significant contributor. Usefulness is a prerequisite to soulful existence; without opportunity to become a true contributor in a community of concern, the drift to emptiness will continue.

One truth, so simple and stark that most academic politicians are unable to grasp it, is that a legitimate society can receive sustenance from *individuals* asserting individual authenticity—that individual presence cannot be ignored and it gives *everyone* a place to begin.

CHAPTER EIGHT

Th-th-they th-th-threw me off th-th-the
d-d-debate t-t-team be-b-because I was
J-J-J-Jewish
OR,
Maybe Nixon didn't win, maybe
McGovern lost

Joe Frazier, after losing an even more one-sided battle to
George Foreman than the presidential election, commented
that he "fought him wrong." Obviously, the same could be
said by George McGovern.

The McGovern campaign, unless understood and analyzed,
could provide the same unfortunate learning that Mark
Twain attributed to a cat who once sat on a hot stove; that
cat never sat on a hot stove again but he also never sat on a
cold one either.

In his campaign, McGovern was handicapped by (1) an
obsession over nonissues, (2) an inability to be clear and congruent about *real* issues, (3) an overwhelming and impossible desire to make the Democratic party *appear* united, and
(4) the ineptness and incompetence of his supporters.

The nonissue that stands out was (as Historians, I'm sure,
will report it) the Eagleton affair. Even now most analysts

report it incorrectly. Some critics fault McGovern and Eagleton for not disclosing a medical history or for inadequate research and a hasty decision, others fault McGovern for his indecisiveness, his proclaimed "one thousand percent" support, and his later buckling under party pressure—that one thousand percent support *was* an indication of inflation that even Richard Nixon couldn't match. None of the above are important. The Eagleton matter was *never* an issue and should *never* have been made one by McGovern. Recall that it was he (and Eagleton) who insisted on a press conference to bare all. In the critical days after the nomination when McGovern *should* have been laying the foundation for his thrust toward the presidency, the headlines blazed forth with only Eagleton's past, real and imagined, and with the communiqués from *that* battlefield everything else paled.

Eagleton's medical history could not have been turned to advantage. Norman Mailer suggested that Eagleton's medical past be featured as an introduction to the redemptive society which McGovern's administration would initiate. That is pure whimsy. There isn't anything politically beneficial about psychiatric treatment, but there is nothing damaging about it either, as Eagleton later proved in his successful bid for reelection to the Senate. Lest *I* be accused of 20-20 hindsight, I would like to present my views of the Eagleton situation *at the time* it was white hot. The Eugene (Oregon) *Register-Guard*, on its front pages, reported my position with all the distortion that makes show business more important than serious analysis in the United States.

> Art Pearl left the public limelight in Eugene Thursday in much the same way he's occupied it for the last seven years —with biting wit and caustic commentary on current events.
> The outspoken University of Oregon education professor and one-time (1970) Democratic gubernatorial candidate is

leaving after seven years on the UO faculty for an administrative position with the University of California at Santa Cruz.

He gave what was billed as his "hail and farewell" speech to Oregon politics Thursday at the weekly Demo Forum luncheon meeting. And he gave members of the jam-packed audience of about 100 what they came to hear.

Some of his scattergunned observations:

● "I was moved to see this many people here today until I remembered that you're probably here to see that I really leave."

● "The Democratic party has become weak, indecisive and over-reacts to nonissues. The only way that party can survive is to provide a clear alternative to what we want this country to look like."

● "It's not important whether our vice presidential candidate was crazy six years ago. The important thing is that the man in the White House is crazy now."

● "We're on an obvious collision course with extinction, unless we change every aspect of our society."

● "The truth is always at the left of center."

● "We can't afford any military budget. The only rational solution is to give General Abrams a dollar and a half and tell him to get out."*

● "The question of whether we have a strong military posture is not relevant. We live in the spaceship Earth and if we blow up any part of it, we blow up the spaceship. The issue of a strong military for protection was probably relevant in 1870 and a reasonable one in 1940. Today, in 1972, it's absurd. Who are our enemies? The only two we talk about are Russia and China, and they've embraced our President."

● "The military is not our only insanity. Unemployment and racism and poverty and war and others also are our insanity."†

● "You can't win elections if you compromise on princi-

* And tell him to knock himself out" (exact quote).
† War on the environment also are our insanities" (exact quote).

193

ple. In fact, you shouldn't win if you compromise on principle."

● "We Democrats have got to take on all the people who are important to the Republican party—the 500 that Fortune Magazine lists each year. All of them represent devastation to us. They represent only 10 companies with $120 billion in sales and $102 billion assets. They all operate out of favorable tax commitments that come out of our hides."

● "We need to make it possible for everyone to have an education from birth to death, for everyone to have meaningful health care. We need to employ millions in Earth-restoring jobs. We need to reorganize our cities. We can't do any of these things unless we differentiate ourselves from the crazies running the country. Nixon represents the poor millionaires. We should represent everyone else."

● "The number one issue this year is that we cannot afford four more years of the destruction of Earth through war, poverty, racism."

● "The Miami convention was the beginning of a new day, a new politics—if we don't back off from that commitment."

● "Mark Hatfield is a good servant of the Republican party and Associated Oregon Industries. The choice in the Senate race this year is between vitality (Wayne Morse) and a very tired old man (Hatfield). It's a choice between someone who made a difference when in the minority and someone who has been an undistinguished politician."

● "The Eagleton affair is a nonissue. A political campaign is not won on the characteristics of the vice presidential candidate. It's won on issues. We should take the initiative to push issues and not over-react to this non-issue. For the first time in a long time, the American people have a clear choice in the direction they want this nation to take."

● "Don't ask me about George Meany. Talk to Frances Scott. She's in charge of the geriatric center at the university. But, don't knock senility. It comes to all of us sooner or later."

● "I have enormous faith in the intelligence of the American people. If we provide an intelligent alternative, they'll make an intelligent decision."

● "If a man doesn't know anything about a job before

194

he's elected to it, he's probably a Democrat. If he doesn't know anything after holding the job for four years, he's a Republican."

● "A vote in democratic politics is really after the fact. The center of democratic politics is a good debate around issues."

Assume that McGovern, rather than wilting, had taken the initiative, allowing the newspaper report to come out without scooping the reporter through a press conference—and suppose that he welcomed discussion of psychiatric symptomatology, by discussing the current insanity of the president. Every time he was accosted by a reporter he would say, "I'm delighted to talk about craziness. I'd like to talk about the military budget and the costs of the bombing, etc.," and lay on a few salient facts. Other times he could take off on economic conditions, environmental matters, health issues—the whole gamut of Nixon inadequacies.

He did none of these things. As a result, he lost initiative and credibility. After he dumped Eagleton, he appeared disloyal and cowardly.

The Watergate affair was another nonissue and before the election *could* not be made into an issue (as was the lack of disclosure of Republican campaign donors). There are a lot of reasons why the Watergate affair was a nonissue. For one thing citizens of the United States are educated (or trained) to expect their political figures to stand tall. Political figures are almost as important as movie stars. Gary Cooper wouldn't whimper if his opponents played dirty, he would face them all at the train station—all alone and outnumbered, and before The End flashed on the screen he would emerge triumphant. John Wayne wouldn't complain because the bad guys play dirty—he would have whipped them into submission, even playing their way if that was necessary. McGovern reduced himself to nonhero status, which is considerably less than villainy. He was the pathetic guy being tormented by black hats who is rescued by the good guys in the nick of time; in the process, he never even wins the girl, so obviously he isn't going to be president.

Making so much out of the Watergate affair gave the impression that the Democrats had something to hide; remember, the American people have been carefully educated to be ignorant about politics, and objecting to spies meant that there were secrets. The notion of a party keeping secrets is as suspicious as an individual asking for the protection of the Fifth Amendment. That Mr. Nixon was involved in secret missions all over the world was O.K. because *he* was king, and kings are allowed secrets, but McGovern's loyalty was suspect anyhow and the fact that he objected to espionage reflected back on both his integrity and his manliness.

The Watergate issue was above all other reasons a nonissue because it was not likely to influence votes. The 30 percent of the votes that McGovern had locked up weren't going to be affected because they knew Nixon to be tricky and, in fact, their value as campaigners was likely to diminish because they would concentrate on that and not on more crucial issues. The other 70 percent couldn't be made to care in time, with the resources available. A proportion of them knew with certainty equal in intensity to the McGovernites that Nixon was above all evildoing and that even suggesting that he could engage in such skullduggery showed how low the opposition could get. And the voters who really mattered, the ones in the middle, were unlikely to care, because many believed that *all* politicians were crooked and, further, there was no way that they could be shown a connection between what went on in Watergate and whether or not they had a job, what groceries cost at the store, how safe was their neighborhood, whether air was breathable, how much taxes they had to pay and what they got for it, whether or not they or their kids had to fight in wars, whether the government frittered away money in welfare, or gave special privileges to nondeserving nonwhites.

McGovern could have used this Watergate espionage case as a political advantage, only by downplaying it, as part of double-entendre humor, tongue-in-cheek ridicule—that kind of a campaign will always bring down a humorless stiff like Richard Nixon. Remember, it is Richard Nixon who has the history of whimpering—and, by taking *that* liability away from him, McGovern dissipated a lot of trumps.

A third nonissue was lack of money for the campaign. Over and over, Lawrence O'Brien and other key McGovern functionaries would lament in public the sorry state of the campaign treasury. The electorate doesn't give a tinker's dam whether one party is rich and the other poor. It would be interesting to them to understand how a party of the rich acted to keep almost everyone poor, but that valuable lesson wasn't learned because it wasn't taught. Rather than getting to the issue of the relationship between political power and wealth, the Democrats altered focus and in that transition McGovern appeared to wallow in self-pity. The image of a pathetic candidate is guaranteed to get the candidate pathetically few votes.

McGovern damaged himself severely when finally he did get down to talking about issues. He had lost the initiative—he had violated Pearl's First Law of Politics, *Get ahead and stay ahead*. He surrendered his advantage in the Eagleton, Watergate, and fund-raising matters, but once he got back on track he floundered again. When he talked about issues, he was fuzzy. He had to back off—he gave the impression that he was unsure of himself. He never communicated how *he* as president would be different than the incumbent.

The weakness of his economic positions has been discussed extensively (see Chapter 6). He came forth with poorly formulated plans from which he backtracked. His guaranteed income plan appeared unsound economically. His approach to work reforms was basically orthodox New Deal. He failed to be specific enough to win converts while his vagueness inspired a lack of confidence.

Even on peace, *the* issue that had distinguished him from his Democratic rivals, he faltered. He lost that when he failed to come forth with a peace plan, when he double-talked about his peace emissary—*his* Kissinger—Pierre Salinger. In fact, on peace he seemed almost to pout and cry much like the child whose toy has been taken away by the bully down the street. Rather than pointing out that Nixon's "peace plans" could not produce a true peace, he stood transfixed as Nixon ran through his Vietnam number. Perhaps McGovern's own confusion about a true peace was reflected in his appearance before the American Legion in late summer. The American Legion convention offered McGovern about the only opportunity he was to have for a head-to-head encounter with his incumbent rival. It would be a chance for *everyone* to see the relative merits of the candidates because the media played it up. At the American Legion convention, McGovern got a chance to strut his stuff the likes of which he never got again.

Nixon did his thing—he was predictable—he oozed confidence, he dropped his platitudes, telling an audience what they desperately wanted to hear. When he spoke of American military might, the audience was brought to almost orgiastic climax. When he spoke of our gallant boys in Vietnam and our prisoners of war we would never betray, tears welled in the eyes of the audience. When he spoke of our homage and our commitment to our veterans, the audience swelled with pride. It was the cocky, brazen performance of a man at home before *his* crowd of warmongering jingoists. When he finished, he got what he knew in advance he would have—a thundering ovation.

Compare this with McGovern. He strode to the podium

with a silly Legion cap cocked on his head and what came out
of his head adequately reflected what he wore. What did he
say? He echoed Nixon's platitudinous sentiments that the
United States must remain the strongest nation in the world
(unenthusiastic applause), that the United States must
increase its benefits to veterans (unenthusiastic applause),
and he reminded the assemblage that he was a fighter pilot in
World War II (silence). He literally groveled before them
—I was not transfixed, but nauseated, by the spectacle emanating from my TV set. As it went, it was all Nixon and if
you had somehow, as a loyal McGovern supporter, maintained another illusion, this was not allowed to you—because
the legionnaires were interviewed after and made it clear
how little they were impressed by McGovern as presidential
material. The appearance before the American Legion was
indicative of the political game McGovern played.

While I writhed before the electronic device that Nixon
has learned to use so well and before which McGovern con-
vincingly established his amateur status I mitigated the pain
through fantasy. I imaged what *I* would have done if I was in
McGovern's place. I would have reasoned that I had no votes
in that audience. The American Legion stood dramatically
opposed to me (and McGovern) on every conceivable issue
—why bother to placate them? Address the larger audience,
the millions whose votes are up for grabs. Start by addressing
them as the "foreign legion" because nothing about them is
American. Tick off their record as war supporters, as opponents of civil rights and liberties, as opponents of ecological,
economic, and every other kind of sanity. Point out that in a
very real sense you are running against the Legion just as
anyone friendly toward them was running against peace,
equality, full employment, and a livable earth, and conclude
by suggesting that there was one thing the Legion could do for
for America—it could disband. Then, in the chorus of boos

199

and other demonstrations of bad manners, triumphantly leave the dais. While you might not have gained a vote, it is possible that Nixon may have lost a few through cardiovascular accidents.

This could have caught fire. This could have established the contrast forcing Nixon to become again the candidate of the atavists forcing him into a position as hardened as the arteries of his supporters—Oh, well.

Because he could not antagonize any segment of the electorate, McGovern in time could not win over any segment either. His campaign was centrifugal; it spun out into a series of indefinite nonpositions. He certainly was not too radical. There was nothing radical about any position he took; there was just a problem deciphering what that position was.

But he did spend a good portion of his campaign complaining about being labeled radical. He pointed out that South Dakota doesn't elect radicals—and, like Hamlet's unfortunate mother, he too "doth protest too much."

In the end, his issues shredded, he asked only to be elected on the basis of his decency (Shirley MacLaine's constant comment), and that wasn't enough.

McGovern's failure to enunciate a coherent platform was related to his desperate efforts to woo back the traditionalists. Thus he courted Dick Daley in Chicago, claiming that only with Dick Daley's support could Illinois be won, and only with Illinois would the United States be won. He welcomed back Hubert Humphrey who, more than any other Democrat, damaged him in the primaries. Apparently, he buckled under to managers of his campaign who reprimanded him for comparing Nixon to Hitler. The sad part of all this is that it gained him nothing; even after his campaign lost character and definition, even after he retreated to the middle, even after he humbled himself before those *he* had vanquished, when it was all over, when *he* paid the ultimate price—it was *they* who turned on *him*.

And this is yet another lesson for those who would forge a Democratic majority out of persons who find it very easy to rise above principle.

McGovern ran a poor campaign—there is no gainsaying that fact. In boxing parlance, he never got off—he was indecisive and he got trapped by nonissues. He didn't do his homework and he got trapped in his calculations, all well and true, and yet others who have done all that and worse have won. McGovern was weakened by his supporters.

The convention which nominated George McGovern on the first ballot was more cosmetic than real. The delegates and tone were different from what people had come to expect from Democratic conventions. The convention was younger, more feminine, darker. Gone from supreme eminence were the handful of king-makers who in closeted secrecy determined the outcome. No one would look at 1972 and suggest that the nomination of president or vice president had to be cleared with a big industrial labor leader—like the late Sidney Hillman of the Amalgamated Clothing Workers or a big city boss like Chicago's Richard Daley. Oh, no! This convention belonged to the people, it was everything that 1968's convention was not. The 1972 Democratic Nominating Convention had one fatal flaw, the same kind of flaw that permeates all modern life in the United States. The convention that nominated George McGovern suffered from a lack of truth in advertising: the youth didn't represent youth, the women did not represent women, the minorities even had a more tenuous hold on their constituencies than was true in less representative conventions. The convention got carried away; they started something they were not prepared to finish. They made implicit commitments in the nominating of George McGovern that they would go ahead and bring under the McGovern banner the persons they purported to represent. This is particularly true of the women and the youth.

In the period of time elapsing between Richard Nixon's ascent to the White House and the Democrats' nominating convention to unseat him, there came into being a significant revival of feminism. Unlike any other oppressed group, women, if they got their "thing" together, could control the political process. They, with 53 percent of the potential votes, could determine the election outcome anywhere; 1972 would reflect how far this movement had come but, like too much of American politics, it was revealed that the women's movement suffered from its rhetoric and a failure to sort out priorities. The movement is handicapped by a lack of specific suggestions which can be translated into political action. This is particularly apparent in the arena of work.

A women's movement must offer a plan for an equitable division of employment—which does not threaten men's opportunity to make a contribution. Women must offer a plan for quality life service for women without threatening service for men.

In addition to specific plans for the future, the women, in generating platform positions designed to reduce exploitation, such as stands on abortion, found themselves in the all-too-familiar position of being too far out in front of their constituencies. Too many women had spoken *for* women without speaking *to* them. As a consequence, with the slickness of all well-managed public relations campaigns, the Nixon steam-roller rolled over the women's leadership and swept into the fold more than half of the women's vote. This is frightening because in every possible respect—from its humor, to its appointments, to its priorities (white with foam?)—the Nixon administration displayed a callous indifference toward women's problems.

- The Nixon administration never saw fit to appoint a woman to either the Supreme Court or the Cabinet. I find it beyond credibility to suggest that there weren't more qualified women than the persons he did appoint to those positions.

- The Nixon administration continued to ask women to fend for themselves (in matters such as child care) while he put more and more of our dollars into such male-dominated enterprises as the military and large-scale business.

- The Nixon administration never used the power of his office for any leadership to alleviate specific problems— the horrendous increase in violent crime against women, the specific problems of aging women, the vulnerability of adolescent girls—all were subjects for benign neglect.

The women's movement, until now, has been an upper-middle-income movement, with some empathy and involvement of the extreme poor; left out are the mass of women who live by their myths and are terrified by the prospects of liberation. These tories are obviously ready to succumb to any new wave of "male-lash" but—unless they are encountered, unless their fears are reordered and their questions answered—they will sneer at any efforts to change the quality of life in the United States. The women's movement (and this has been carefully fostered by its enemies) appears to many as more anti-male than pro-female; often, it is also reduced to a reform of manners, which is not sufficient to get many people involved. But the movement moved! There were modest gains for women. An additional five women were elected to the House of Representatives (this gain was only slightly offset by loss of the lone woman in the Senate). This advance was in the Democratic party. The Democratic party is much less committed to a sexist distribution of power and wealth than is the Republican party. This truth has escaped too many women, particularly in the backwash of its "male-lash," reflected in a series of tracts which argue that females really dominate males, that females really control all the wealth, that females are too mature to be involved in the childish male games of business, war, and politics, and assorted other flimflam. Politically aware women are going to have to find mechanisms to locate and communicate to women who vote for the Richard Nixons. It will, of course, be much easier if the men who control the Democratic party generate programs with substance to aid such conversations.

The youth, even more than women, were caught up in rhetoric. The young people who rallied behind McGovern were unable to make contact with the vast majority of persons under the age of 25 and even those under the age of 21. It was curious how persons under the age of 21, ignored by the Republican party and even exploited for political gain, became a valuable commodity to be captured. As soon as the 18-year-old had a vote, the Republican party changed its appearance even to the point of lengthening hair style and shortening its liturgy. Here, again, was an effort to try to present a stimulus that would attract a vote source nonexistent before and against which the McGovernites, who had staked the prior claim, were unable to respond.

The campus-bound youth ran into problems when they found they had really very little to say and not much language to say it with in their encounters with youth in factories, taverns, pool halls, and on motorcycles. As a consequence, they ran back to the campus where they felt comfortable albeit impotent. The youth on campus with access to information and time to formulate alternatives had best find ways to share both with less favored young people or else they too might find themselves in reduced straits.

The McGovern program failed to fly for many, many reasons. Not the least important was the disconnectedness of the support. The campaign began as a political alliance of women, youth, eco-freaks, eggheads, emancipated blue-collar workers, peaceniks, and minorities. All were riding pet hobby horses. It is not surprising that the coalition fell apart. It had no intellectual glue. By 1976 this group, which has the potential to sweep the land, will have to work out its thoughts until it becomes a coordinated whole—otherwise, disaster again.

The McGovern campaign fell apart because too much was attempted too soon. The aftermath of 1968 took its toll for too long and, when finally aroused from the lethargy of disillusionment, too many necessary steps were bypassed, too much was taken for granted, and too fragile a foundation was laid.

There is no retreat. The alternative of a Committee for a Democratic Majority *way back thar* is a Committee for a Democratic Majority *up front now*. The McGovern campaign was a start in the correct direction; it was undermined by nonissues, weak statements of issues, efforts toward unreal alliances, and poorly prepared supporters. These are all remediable defects.

And that's the lesson to be learned from George McGovern. He made mistakes; who hasn't? But he got something going and, for all the weaknesses, *that* should never be forgotten.

CHAPTER NINE

The boys in the bandwagon
OR,
A slick poll-ish joke

In basketball or hockey, the person who makes it possible for another to score is credited with an assist. The public opinion pollsters deserve such accreditation for their contribution to the Richard Nixon victory, and because of that they create yet another challenge for a working democracy. Public opinion survey corporations influence elections in three vital ways: (1) they create a bandwagon effect and act like a light for political tropisms—and, in *close* elections, this alone is sufficient to alter the balance; (2) they influence the packaging of the candidate, and thus they limit and distort what the electorate is allowed to know; and (3) they discourage the campaigners for the underdog, particularly if their favorite seems hopelessly behind, and hope is the energy force that keeps an underdog campaign alive.

Polls have been a factor in U.S. elections for a long time. Their credibility was shaken in 1936 with the magnificent error of the *Literary Digest* in heralding an Alf Landon victory and again in 1948 when they were narrowly wrong in forecasting Thomas Dewey's election—but their impact has been there and has constantly been gaining in importance. Polling techniques have become more sophisticated: analysis, because of the availability of computers, can be more penetrating and yet, most critical of all, the candidate can be shaped to fit the mold of the opinion and reshaped to fit the shifting sands of public opinion. All of this gives more power to those who need power the least and makes the problems of reform politics all the more difficult.

Public opinion polls are real and upon us and there is only a limited number of responses to them. One approach is to, in effect, concede to them, and generate sets of candidates who are carbon copies of the incumbents, only slightly better merchandised; elections that become mere advertising campaigns in which the electorate is given a choice between Gillette or Schick to cut their throats. This is what I believe the Committee for a Democratic Majority is really up to: to find policies and people who coincide with current prejudices. This form of politics, even if successful, would destroy any validity in the democratic process and would further undermine an already undermined leadership function. Given the distribution of resources of both major parties, it is highly unlikely that the Democrats would win too many important posts—and, even if they did, their action would change but slightly the quality of life of the poor and other beaten-down classes.

Another approach would be to curtail public opinion polls as enemies of the democratic process. It is hardly likely that any proscriptive legislation could be passed; why, indeed, would the people in power who got where they are through reliance on this process turn on their benefactors? And even if legislation was passed it would be unenforceable, leading to "underground polls," more readily available to those in power than to challengers. If agents of the Republican party are going to use wiretaps, they would certainly use any other device to aid their cause. But even if bans and restrictions were possible and could be enforced, this would be the wrong way to go. Polls are merely symbols and symptoms of more basic flaws of a society—cracks in the foundation—and new wallpaper won't keep the house from falling apart.

The only real solution to the possible negative influence of polls is to educate people to live above them. In fact, every threat to a democracy, when boiled down to its essence, is merely a device to take advantage of voter ignorance. An ignorant voter is a voter asking to be duped. All that the polls do is to reduce the fooling process to a science—that's no great accomplishment. Return to the three impacts that the polls had on the McGovern-Nixon debacle: seducing the voters to back the winner; tailoring Nixon to fit, and production of feelings of hopelessness in McGovern supporters. All can be dealt with at a more basic level.

Voting for a winner solely because he is to be the winner is by far the most primitive motivation for a vote; it is a reflection of a desperate search for identification and gratification and should be interpreted that way. The only hope for a democracy is that this kind of voting is reduced to insignificance and *that* can be done only through some form of education of the mass. The bandwagon effect is thus much less a statement of what voters *do* than it is a statement of what political educators *do not* do. The incidence of the "vote for the winner" syndrome will be reduced in direct proportion to the amount of "thinking" that goes on whenever human beings gather; since the theme has been extended throughout many of the previous pages, no more need be presented here.

The packaging of candidates to popular demand is a much more serious and difficult problem. The most learned among us can be deceived by promises of derring-do ahead and by a record of seemingly glittering past accomplishments, particularly as highly selective facts are sprinkled about to create one illusion after another. The fooling of the learned becomes ever easier as the sciences are more and more specialized and compartmentalized and as blandishments are tendered scholars of the correct political persuasion. College professors use deodorants as talismans to keep their families safe from harm, so why shouldn't they just as readily be seduced by election promises? As with everything else in the world, and this is especially true in politics, there are no iron-clad guaranteed remedies for the perversion of politics through false advertising, but accountable leadership certainly could help. That leadership would be willing to debate in every market place the merits of different policies, allocations of resources, and so on. In this debate, terms owned by privileged "elites" must become public domain. The voter really has no choice if he or she is *not allowed* to know what politicians are talking about because the language is a secret code. True intellectual leadership translates obscure theory and relationships into concepts that are universally understandable. True intellectual leadership struggles to be heard on TV or radio or in newspapers. This just hasn't been happening in the last few decades and the net result is that it is easier to bamboozle a public with big words now than ever before *and* the image of intellectual leadership is continually deflated. True intellectual debate has to be introduced in place of the childish displays of bad manners and no content that currently hold sway in programs MC'd by William F. Buckley and other knownothings.

Being declared the loser by the polls is not universally disastrous. The United States loves an underdog. So much of our romantic tradition is wrapped in rooting the underdog on to victory. There is excitement in dramatic come-from-behind victories. But McGovern was denied even that part of a potential dialectical force. The Nixon folks, leaving nothing to chance, had carefully manufactured the underdog role for themselves. Over the years they emphasized how they stood up courageously almost alone against the attacks of such bullies as *The New York Times* and the SDS. Valiant is the word for Richard became the *sotto voce* slogan of the early campaign until the reverberations of subliminal effects developed into a deafening crescendo. Over and over in one form and another, images were projected of a brave and solitary Richard M. Nixon standing firm and resolute while louts were nipping at his heels—the picture I like best is of him standing in the freezing cold in the boat crossing the Delaware. Like everything else not bolted down, Richard Nixon stole the underdog role but, even if he had not been successful, it would have been difficult for McGovern to have won it. The United States loves an underdog—except when he is subversive. Nobody loves a subversive, even subversives' mothers don't love them (that's probably why they become subversive, say the psychologists among us). Very neatly and all so subtly, McGovern's patriotism was constantly challenged—never directly in the old Nixon tradition, but indirectly in the new Nixon tradition—by denying continually that any such aspersions could be cast on McGovern himself, but the president's supporters were not restricted and were allowed to take issue with their leader (which goes to show just how big he is). So suspicions were sowed about:

- McGovern's engaging in independent international diplomatic relationships with his personal emissary Pierre Salinger.
- how McGovern's offices were used to plan illegal activities against the president (although after the election people associated with Richard Nixon's campaign were found guilty of such behavior).
- how McGovern's historical past was shaky and shady.

If there are to be polls which establish favorites and underdogs, it is important that in an educational campaign a public be educated on how candidates use and manipulate those designations for political advantage.

There is yet another aspect of polls which must be considered as part of the lathe that shapes a candidate. Polls don't merely sample opinion, they also change and create opinions. The pollsters are never neutral, they are not noble referees knocking on doors merely requesting facts, ma'am. Pollsters have axes to grind and they feel loyalties to patrons. In a great many instances, questions are phrased to get people to think about things that had not entered their minds or to think differently about issues. The polls become sneaky ways to set up a public for a policy shift. This aspect of opinion survey isn't just an irrelevant observation to serve as filler—trivia for the social psychologist. The knowledge that public opinion outfits *create* opinion has practical significance in that (1) the information provides clues to the strategy of the opponent; watching the outputs of *his* pollsters in residence prepares *you* for where he is going; and (2) this information reaffirms what you should always remember: in a politically disinterested society, such as ours has become, opinions are tentative and fragile and anything that easily altered can be changed again, and again, and again.

How to keep your hope when all about are losing theirs

Those in the frightening and lonely business of trying to change the warp and woof of U.S. politics don't need any further discouragement, and polls take away the comforting distortion that comes from selective contacts. In this sense, the polls are destructive, but only to people with very immature notions of what they are about. There weren't any polls around in 1850 to tell Wendell Phillips that his views about abolition were unpopular—he got that message from the way the public jeered and hooted and from the fact that his life and property were constantly threatened. Polls can be a source of support, because they provide a form of feedback to be used to alter tactics and reevaluate strategy.

The major reason underdogs become discouraged is that they are taken with the infantile notion that winning is everything. The ultimate change in a society comes not from the vote outcome but the nature of the debate; in this context, polls provide valuable information, indicating, for example, the loss that takes place between the transmission of ideas and their reception by different audiences. In politics the true joy is in participation. If this can't be understood, a workable just political system would not survive either the exhilaration that accompanies winning or the despondency that comes with defeat.

There is a curious distortion of the *winning-is-everything* thesis and that is the *winning-is-nothing* argument. Here we find grotesque theatre replacing true political involvement; the polls don't influence this kind of activity because there is no desire to respond to where people are—although the "politicians" not concerned with winning do believe that they are involved in political education. They are deceiving themselves. All significant political activity *is directed at winning*; unless there is some hope of winning, the "education" becomes sloppy, empty, and even negative. The aim *must* be to win, but never winning at all costs (something I believe the Committee for a Democratic Majority may be guilty of) or winning as an end detached from the excitement of the campaign. When politics is seen as an unending campaign with the election as a subgoal, neither the pollsters nor anyone else can take hope away.

As deliriously happy as the president himself were the professional poll takers. They received accolades for being right on the button. Applause for them may be as unearned as applause for the president. Both happen to be significant obstacles that a politically aware people will just have to work around.

CHAPTER TEN

Watergate–the blot that wouldn't go away
OR,
The last tangle on the Potomac

Less than six months after his greatest triumph, after attaining the pinnacle of pinnacles, Richard Nixon came tumbling down looking very much like the Humpty Dumpty he had worked so hard all his life not to be; Richard Nixon met his downfall at the Watergate Apartments and all the big money and all the party men couldn't put him back together again. At least so it seemed back in those exhilarating, halcyon late May days of 1973.

How did it happen? How did the nonissue of the November campaign—one of the many political pebbles that McGovern stumbled over—grow to such importance in so short a time?

How could Robert Dole, the now ex-chief of the Republican party, so lugubrious on election night, reach an even lower low in late April stating then that the Republican party as the consequence of Watergate had "zero credibility"?

215

How could Spiro Agnew's former press secretary Victor Gold conclude that the wrong people won in 1972? Gold reached this conclusion by dismissing the excuse that the president was misled by those around him,

> as a banality of an order that conservative Republicans generally expect from liberal Democrats. . . . In short, President Nixon should have known the extent to which those he trusted were capable of advising their delegated power. If that is too much to ask them and help us, we were wrong and the McGovernites, in their quintessential philosophy, were right. The system is bad, and so long as it exists, nobody is responsible for anything. Pass the grass. (Quoted in Great Falls (Montana) *Tribune*, May 2, 1973)

The anguish of some, the exultation of others, the meaning and the meaningless of Watergate can only be understood against the backdrop of the known occurrences of that celebrated affair. These were the *unassailable facts* on May 1, the day after President Nixon publicly acknowledged, took full responsibility and *no blame* for the hanky panky of Watergate and subsequent events.

Phase 1: Political entymology

June 17, 1972

Police arrest five men—Bernard L. Barker, Eugene R. Martin, Frank A. Sturgis, James W. McCord and Virgilio R. Gonzales—for breaking into the Democratic National Committee offices on the sixth floor of the Watergate apartments in Washington, D.C.

June 19, 1972

McCord dismissed from his post as chief security officer for Committee for the Re-election of the President (CRP).

June 19, 1972

Presidential counsel John W. Dean appointed to investigate incident.

June 19, 1972

Presidential press secretary Ron Ziegler called "the break-in" "a third-rate burglary attempt" and something "that should not fall into the political process."

June 20, 1972

John W. Mitchell, former Attorney General and now campaign manager for Richard Nixon, calls million-dollar suit filed by Democratic Party Chief Lawrence O'Brien against CRP "another example of political demagoguery."

June 21, 1972

John Mitchell "deplores" the break-in as did National Chairman Robert Dole.

June 22, 1972

President Nixon pronounced officially that "the White House has no involvement whatever in the particular incident."

June 28, 1972

Gordon Liddy fired as attorney for CRP for ostensibly refusing to cooperate with FBI inquiry of Watergate.

July 1, 1972

Mitchell quits as Nixon campaign manager for "family reasons."

Phase 2: The Republican counterattack

"It's a long, long time from June to November" and as the days grow shorter, the Republicans take the initiative by suggesting that the Demos are low-lifes for interjecting Watergate into the democratic process—

—However, things to remember in August, September and October were:

August 25, 1972

Maurice H. Stans, former Secretary of Commerce, now chief fund-raiser for Nixon campaign, is questioned in Miami about $114,000 campaign funds that apparently ended up in the hands of Watergate intruder Bernard Barker.

August 28, 1972

Attorney General Richard Kleindienst pledged Justice Department to a "most intensive, thorough and comprehensive investigation," one which "no fair-minded person would say that we whitewashed or dragged our feet on it."

August 29, 1972

Richard Nixon, on the basis of Dean's investigation, pronounced "no one on the White House staff, no one in this administration, presently employed [thus excluding those already arrested] was involved in this bizarre incident."

September 1, 1972

John Mitchell swears that he "had no advance knowledge of the bugging incident."

September 13, 1972

The Republican Party files $2.5 million dollar countersuit against Lawrence O'Brien, charging Democrats with using federal courts "as instrument for creating political headlines."

September 15, 1972

Original Watergate Five plus Gordon Liddy and Howard Hunt indicted by Federal Grand Jury in Washington, D.C.

September 19, 1972

Watergate Seven plead not guilty before Chief U.S. District Judge John J. Sirica.

October 10, 1972

Washington Post story charges Watergate to be part of a "massive campaign of political spying and sabotage" and identifies Donald H. Segretti as recruiter of saboteurs and spies. (Outraged self-righteous denial by Republicans everywhere including the president's press secretary Ron L. Ziegler)

October 18, 1972

Ron L. Ziegler responds to question with a refusal "to dignify with comment stories based on hearsay, character assassination, innuendo or guilt by association."

October 19, 1973

Jeb Stuart Magruder, (a deputy director of Committee for Re-election of the President and later implicator of John Mitchell and counsel to the president John Dean as Watergate planners), in *Time*: "Listen, when this is all over you'll know that there were only seven people who knew about the Watergate, and they are the seven who were indicted by the grand jury."

October 28, 1973

Ron L. Ziegler blasts the report that the president's chief of staff, H. R. Haldeman, controlled a secret fund for espionage and sabotage as "shabby journalism. . . . a blatant effort at character assassination. . . . Mr. Dean informed me that there was no secret fund."

November 7, 1972

Election Day.

December 8, 1972

Mrs. E. Howard Hunt, wife of Watergate defendant, killed in airline crash. Found in her possession were $10,000 in hundred-dollar bills.

Phase 3: Tune out for trial and the end to loyalty -- or, they just don't make spies and saboteurs as they used to

January 8, 1973

Watergate trial begins.

January 12, 1973

Hunt pleads guilty to all charges.

January 15, 1973

Barker, Martin, Sturgis and Gonzales plead guilty.

January 30, 1973

Jury finds McCord and Liddy guilty of all eight counts of conspiracy, burglary and wiretapping.

February 2, 1973

Judge Sirica charges that all facts not disclosed in Watergate trial.

February 7, 1973

Senate by a 77-0 vote creates select committee headed by North Carolinian Sam Ervin, Jr., to investigate Watergate.

February 28, 1973

L. Patrick Gray, acting FBI chief, testifies that he made FBI files on Watergate available to White House.

March 8, 1973

L. Patrick Gray testifies that John W. Dean was present when FBI questioned White House aides on Watergate.

March 15, 1973

President Nixon creates unprecedented executive privilege and thereby prevents Dean from testifying before Senate Judiciary Committee

Phase 4: The house of cards gets higher and higher

March 21, 1973

President Nixon announces, just eight months short of one day after he first denied any White House involvement, a White House investigation of Watergate.

March 23, 1973

Judge John J. Sirica sentences Watergate defendants to long prison terms: Liddy, 6½ to 20 years in prison; Hunt, 40 years; McCord, sentence postponed.

March 23, 1973

McCord testifies that he and others were "under pressure to plead guilty and remain silent," thus allowing others involved to escape.

March 24, 1973

McCord tells Senate probers that Dean and Magruder knew about Watergate in advance.

March 24, 1973

Ron L. Ziegler responds as follows to McCord testimony about Dean: "It is totally false that Mr. Dean had prior knowledge of the Watergate matter."

March 24, 1973

Richard M. Nixon quoted by Senate minority leader Hugh Scott: "I have nothing to hide—the White House has nothing to hide, and you are authorized to make that statement in my name."

March 26, 1973

Ron L. Ziegler, after L. Patrick Gray testifies before Senate Judiciary Committee that Dean "probably lied" . . . "We do not associate ourselves with any involvement that suggests that Mr. Dean probably lied."

March 29, 1973

John Mitchell, "I deeply resent the slanderous and false statement about me concerning the Watergate matter reported as being based on hearsay and leaked out. I have previously denied any prior knowledge of or any involvement in the Watergate affair and again reaffirm such denials."

March 30, 1973

Richard Nixon gives up executive privilege and orders all staff to cooperate with grand jury.

Phase 5: When April showers come along, canaries sing their song

April 4, 1973

Liddy given eighteen months additional contempt sentence by Judge Sirica for refusing to answer questions about Watergate.

April 6, 1973

John Dean corroborates much of McCord's accusations in discussions with Watergate prosecutors.

April 11, 1973

Robert Riesner, Magruder's chief assistant, also corroborates McCord statement in testimony before grand jury.

April 14, 1973

Jeb Magruder goes to Justice Department and claims that John Mitchell approved plans for the espionage and that Dean and Mitchell approved efforts to buy silence of Watergate defendants.

April 14, 1973

Mitchell goes to Washington to "officially" confer with Erhlichman, although Martha Mitchell "insists that" the former Attorney General had actually met with the president and that she and her husband were being set up "as the two culprits."

April 17, 1973

Richard Nixon announces that "if any person in the executive branch of the government is indicted by the Grand Jury, my policy will be to immediately suspend him."

April 17, 1973

Ron L. Ziegler proclaims "the President's statement today is the operative statement" and that previous statements "are inoperative."

April 20, 1973

John Mitchell admits to Grand Jury that he had sat in on discussions about Watergate espionage but insists that he vetoed all such proposals.

April 27, 1973

Gray resigns as acting director of FBI, admitting that he destroyed, at the insistence of Dean and presidential chief domestic adviser John D. Ehrlichman, Watergate files taken from the safe of Howard Hunt.

April 30, 1973

Ehrlichman and H. R. Haldeman resign. Dean is fired.

May 1, 1973

Ziegler publicly apologizes to *Washington Post*.

There you have it—and what does it all mean? How could I add more to a matter on which everyone has said so much and perhaps contributed so little. All points of view seem to converge on Watergate. There are those on the left, right and middle who criticize the president and there are those who criticize the critics. Among the latter is—predictably—William Buckley. His broadsides against Arthur Schlesinger, Jr., reflect so much of the confusions of a grating society.

Arthur Schlesinger takes the tack that the president in his actions at Watergate revealed himself to be either a fool or rogue and that either would be sufficient grounds for removal from office. Buckley responds by chastising Schlesinger for his lack of originality. (*That* accusation is indeed strange coming from Mr. Buckley, who never said anything that wasn't first and better uttered by Little Orphan Annie.) Buckley, without reliance on either logic or evidence, exonerates Mr. Nixon from malfeasance and then just as imperiously he dismisses the allegation that Richard Nixon is a fool by (a) arguing that Schlesinger is a fool, and (b) by insisting that Richard Nixon is merely loyal and loyalty is not the badge of fools. Here then is Watergate from pomposity's head:

> On the assumption that we are driven to the second of Mr. Schlesinger's alternatives by the simple act of rejecting the first, then Mr. Nixon is a fool. But what does that make Mr. Schlesinger? Richard Nixon outwitted the Democratic Party first in 1968 and then in 1972, defeating the candidate of the Democratic Party whom Arthur Schlesinger went out of his way to anoint.

But to prepare for more systematic discussion, let's dispense with Mr. Buckley's nonsense. Whether Schlesinger is or is not a fool is a matter of complete insignificance, since

Schlesinger is not president, Nixon is. Assuming that both Nixon and Schlesinger are fools, both should be in the same place—out of the White House.

Now to the more serious charge—the responsibility of a president for his underlings. Was Nixon misled by his or not, or is this even the most important aspect of l'affaire Watergate?

Watergate might become clearer if the momentous issues that surround it are analyzed in some order.

To make sense out of all that noise and confusion, it might be helpful to sort out comment into two distinct arenas of relevance. These are: the failure of a system and the betrayal of a system.

Failure of a system

For Watergate to happen, something was wrong somewhere, and identifying *the* principle cause or causes became a favorite occupation for political analysts. Almost, without exception, such commentators attributed the affair to phenotypic origins and on the basis of that diagnosis advocated minor repairs to an otherwise healthy body politic. To these "experts" Watergate was the equivalent of a flat tire that a little patching here and there would make as good as new. So we find recommended better corrupt practices laws, a less encapsulated White House organization, ceilings on campaign expenditures, and limiting the president to one six-year term. Typical expression of these sentiments came from Secretary of HEW "Cap" Weinberger. He, like so many others speaking *for* the president, first apologized for previous laxities vis-à-vis Watergate, *then* he proposed remedies, and *finally* he warned about making so much of the matter.

> So Mr. Weinberger admitted he was "silly" for "dismissing" Watergate as "essentially ephemeral" and allowed that "I shouldn't have commented on something I didn't know any-

thing about." Then he resolutely got to the periphery of the matter by advocating that "highest priority" be given to reforming the electoral system in the form of "sharp limitation" on campaign contributions to candidates, and he concluded by stating that the "real scandal" would occur if criticism of Watergate led to the scuttling of Nixon's basic domestic policies. *(San Francisco Chronicle,* May 18, 1973)

Now there is issue-clouding at its very best. The "real scandal" of the Nixon administration *is* its "domestic policies"—a point which I have stressed throughout the book. Those domestic policies markedly increase threats of war, threaten the environment, reinforce race and class bias and lock people into poverty.

Those domestic policies distort all government to serve the narrow selfish interests of a privileged few at the expense of the vast majority. Those domestic policies lead to "energy crises," "inflation," "unemployment," "inferior governmental service." Those domestic policies produce crime in the streets almost at the same pace as crime in the nation's government is revealed, or, as many were heard to say, they took crime out of the streets and brought it into the White House. The Casper Weinberger thesis is to be expected. After all, he does serve at the pleasure of the president, but persons not in any way connected (at least not visibly) to the commander in chief come up with similar arguments.

Joseph Kraft, for example, ponders the true meaning of government and laments, in a manner reminiscent of Halberstam, its impact on *this* administration's "Best and Brightest." Kraft identifies the problem as corruption of government.

> The more we learn about Watergate the more we understand that it is not primarily a political scandal growing out of campaign practices. It is primarily a governmental scandal growing out of a corrupt system.
>
> Some of the best men in Washington, including Henry

Kissinger, General Alexander Haig and Richard Helms have been compromised. Their passive acceptance of dirty tricks had nothing to do with politics or the 1972 campaign.

Kraft contends that Kissinger, Haig and Helms all got dirtied with the bugging of National Security Council senior associate Morton Halperin's private telephone, and that Helms was less than honest when early in the Watergate investigations he cleared the CIA of any responsibility. Kraft concludes:

> The point of all this is not that Kissinger, Haig and Helms are bad men. They are not. They are the best the country has to offer.
> But the fact that officials of their caliber can be compromised by Watergate is a gauge of how much reform is necessary. It is not a matter of changing campaign laws or firing half a dozen men or even impeaching the President. What has to be changed is the whole spirit of government.

A spirit of government isn't changed until the locus and focus of the *new* government is defined, and that definition Kraft and his colleagues in the fourth estate have steadfastly refused to come up with. Until there is more substance in the rhetoric of the critics of government there *can* be no change, and that is an important, if not the most important, lesson to be learned from Watergate.

If Kraft is too vague and poetical in his remedies, Kevin P. Phillips, a former Nixon aide turned columnist, is hardly that. Phillips sees the problem in governmental mechanisms and claims that the United States is suffering from hardening of the arteries and needs basic reform in delegation of powers.

> To marshal executive-branch power on behalf of his "New American Revolution," President Nixon is necessarily trying to end-run not only Congress but the bureaucratic structure built up under the Democrats from 1933 to 1966. Federal management is being centralized in the White House under the aegis of a "supercabinet," efficiency experts

226

and advertising men. Under our "separation of powers," Presidential aides have "executive privilege" not to testify before Congress. The result: an unprecedented, unreachable elite managerial cadre in the office of the President. . . .

Might not the answer lie in a *fusion of powers* tying Congress and the executive together, eliminating checks and balances and creating a new system? In a parliamentary regime, our present sort of paralysis would be impossible. Budgeting and spending would be coordinated. Interest groups and lobbies would lose access. Congress would open up to more talent. So would the executive branch. Obligatory interaction with party legislators—to say nothing of parliamentary question periods—would curb the growth of a secretive White House managerial elite.

What the Phillipses of the world close *their* eyes to is that crises in government run far *deeper* than they allow themselves to consider. The issue runs to the basic understanding of people about government. Rearranging power among those who misrepresent people will but slightly alter corruption or other misfeasances.

The issue is not that Mr. Nixon and/or his associates were irresponsible. The issue is that a "free" people voted a person so spectacularly unqualified to be president to the office—*twice!* The second time by a landslide. That is the issue, and given that as the issue, the notion that a one six-year term in office would remedy matters borders on black humor—the six-year plan is the president's own suggestion (and one which he could personally implement by resigning at the end of 1974). It has no true merit because a Committee to Elect a President could, with sufficient funds and disregard for decency, sabotage and spy to the same degree to elect the president the first time as they did to reelect him.

Corruption in government is the direct result of ignorance and indifference in the electorate. The Watergate affair reflects the failure of education so often discussed in these pages. Every public education system must share some blame in Watergate. Every educational system must also assume some responsibility for future consequences.

The press has contorted itself beyond recognition in self-praise over its Watergate activities. Perhaps they should be more modest. The persistent diligence of *Washington Post* reporters Robert Woodward and Carl Bernstein in digging away at Watergate should be applauded (as indeed they were with Pulitzer Prizes and big book publishing advances) but theirs was only a small part of the educational activity, and even these activities were localized, limited in scope to the kind of scandal that titillates readers of Hollywood gossip columns. The newspapers did little more than describe. There was no true discussion and only the most tentative suggestions, despite the headlines. Dick Tracy and Steve Canyon were still the major influences shaping or reflecting policy at home and abroad.

William Randolph Hearst, Jr., illustrated the weakness of the press in an editorial, "The President's Dilemma" (May 6, 1973). In this essay, Hearst condemned the White House isolation from the press, chided the President for his weak performance in his April 30 speech and in that criticism, Hearst had harsh words for his long-time friend.

> I'm afraid the President not only has had faulty communication with his White House staff but with the American people as well, who want and deserve a more decisive executive reaction to Watergate than they have gotten.
>
> For a change, I must agree with at least part of a generally hostile article written on the subject by Arthur Schlesinger Jr. in the Wall Street Journal.

And for all his belated fault finding, Hearst's conclusion to his piece was mind-blowing:

> Persons trying to understand why Mr. Nixon took so long to speak up and do something about Watergate made the point that originally, at least, he must have regarded what

little he was told as evidence of continuing personal attack by such liberal papers as the Washington Post and N.Y. Times. To him it was all part of the same old vendetta against him—nothing more.

There may well be something in this. I'm inclined to think, as a matter of fact, that if the Watergate scandal had been broken by the Hearst Newspapers he would have paid a lot more attention than he did.

That is the logic that Nixon himself used to explain how Watergate grew and grew. Nixon understandably and even legitimately may view the *Washington Post* with suspicion. But why then did the Hearst press hang back? Why didn't they, with their vast resources, get into the investigation independently? Why didn't Mr. Hearst, with his long history of Nixon friendship and influence, try to break down the walls of isolation and let the truth in? He owed it to his friend; he owed it to the country. The Hearst statement is very much like the Nixon statement—a disclaimer of blame. It won't do, particularly when the Hearst press has done as much to build up the Nixon Image.

Another public educator and old friend of the president, the Reverend Billy Graham, also seems to get a wee bit confused about his responsibilities in the Watergate affair. In effect, Mr. Graham comes up with the ultimate alibi for the president—he updates and only slightly modifies the age-old excuse: "The devil made him do it." That's not quite what Billy Graham said. This is:

> The Watergate affair, however, is but a symptom of the deeper moral crisis that affects the nation. On every level of our society, public and private, deceit, dishonesty and moral looseness seem to be increasing. A taxi driver in one of our largest cities said to me recently, "This whole city is corrupt."
>
> The time is overdue for Americans to engage in some deep soul-searching about the underpinnings of our society and our goals as a nation. For decades we have been brain-

washed into thinking that there are no absolute moral standards. Many people have said that man is simply the product of his environment and therefore is not really responsible for his actions. We are now reaping the bitter fruits of these teachings. As a result, the very moral fiber of our society is in grave danger of being shredded. What can we do? Where can we turn? Is it too late? These are some of the questions that millions of Americans are now asking. (*San Francisco Chronicle*, May 20, 1973)

Mr. Graham then quotes, from Nehemiah 8:1-3, a phrase that has the words "water gate" in it and tells us that's what will lead us out of the Watergate and similar messes.

What Mr. Graham says about decline of moral standards is certainly amply documented, but has he really said all that needs to be said? It is certainly true we "live in a society too often dominated by selfish interests and expediency." But who has been among the most consistent spokesman for such selfish interests and expediency? Mr. Nixon certainly has as good a set of credentials as anybody. And don't we have a right to expect some moral leadership from our president? And doesn't a moral leader like Mr. Graham have an obligation to demand that from his long-time friend?

Betrayal of a system

Much has been made of the possibility that those closest to the president betrayed him (and the rest of us) by acting without the president's awareness. These persons, Dean, Mitchell, Magruder, Gray, Segretti, McCord, et al. (and perhaps Ehrlichman and Haldeman), when viewed sympathetically, are seen as overzealous patriots, but even Barry Goldwater has come to realize that "extremism in defense of liberty *is* a crime."

Even when the saboteurs and spies (and those that sanctioned and paid them) are not granted lofty motives, the president is very often exonerated. He is not expected to be on top of such "dirty tricks" because he is so busy with his great works—"ordering bombing," "visiting far-off lands," "lowering prices," and "creating employment."

The president in his pronouncements tries both arguments. He claims he has been fearfully busy. In his April 30 speech he states that on fateful June 17 he was "in Florida trying to get a few days rest after my visit to Russia." But it must be remembered that he returned from Russia on June 2, so perhaps a major difficulty is that Mr. Nixon lacks the vitality for the strenuous job of president, and if that is so, then he can be removed under provisions of the 25th amendment of the Constitution.

The president also invokes the cause of national security and the need for vigilance as justification for the extralegal behavior of those closest to him. There is undoubtedly a need for a U.S. intelligence system, but the already powerful existing FBI and CIA hardly need augmentation by the likes of the crew who have been exposed in Watergate. Those attached to the White House have not distinguished themselves as anything other than "bunglers," as yet another old friend of the president, Murry Chotiner, is quick to point out. He is quoted by London *Observer* columnist Michael Davie thus:

> "They reached the top too fast without seasoning or training—those aren't the people in there who've had the political experience. —Nothing is more arrogant than youth." (*San Francisco Chronicle*, April 29, 1973)

Arrogance is certainly a factor but the betrayal of a president and a country cannot be attributed to mere callowness. Intelligence in today's world may be a necessity, but when sabotage and espionage of the major opposition party is exculpated on those grounds, the excuses even more than the acts become betrayals of a free society.

Public response to Watergate is completely consistent with

the phenomenological cost-benefit analysis presented previously. Personal decisions about Watergate are made on the basis of psychological gratifications of security, comfort, belonging, usefulness, competence and meaning that are attached to those decisions.

People will go to great lengths to deceive themselves. They don't want to appear stupid or foolish nor do they relish the costs of citizen responsibility. To avoid stupidity, it is easier to let experts do the thinking; to avoid responsibility, it is cheaper to delegate those duties to the president.

Now those bargain basement decisions are being challenged, many people have invested heavily in their belief systems. To give them up could mean loss of friends, loss of belief in one's own intellectual competence, loss of the ability to make sense of the world, and various other aches and pains. So as the president becomes less credible, the belief in him in many gains strength with the energy of desperation.

There is yet another reason that people remain loyal to the president. He helps that along by the way he organizes their impression of him. This is something that psychologist Harry Helson calls Adaptation Level. Simply put, adaptation level is the mechanism whereby the organism attains a new equilibrium when challenged with new stimuli. Any stimuli confronting an organism will cause it to either move toward or move away. By and large, the organism will move toward the average of all stimuli confronting it. Group pressures constitute important forces acting on an individual and can influence whether a stimulus is rejected or accepted.

The applicability of the above to the president is relatively clear—he works very hard to field-test whether his statements will be accepted or rejected (e.g. "China," "Cambodia," "New Economic Policy"). In Watergate, he was clearly in trouble, so he staged his responses and developed three levels of adaptation—the first step was denial of everything (that stabilized the population) ; the second step was accepting full responsibility (that was designed to pull them slightly to him) ; the third step was to admit knowledge of the affair, but claiming that it was only in the interests of national security (that is taking the initiative and increasing the equilibrium) ; the fourth step is likely to attack the patriotism or fairness of his critics. If he started with the first, given the country's mood, he would have been rejected and the new equilibrium established as a result might have moved beyond his influence.

An example of successful sequencing of adaptation levels is found in Nazi Germany where "liberal" persons went through a set of "changes" from hostility to acceptance of Hitler without ever consciously considering the steps they were taking.

Watergate is, in truth, a symptom of both a hurting society and a corrupt political regime. It should not be analyzed out of context. The corruption is not limited to electioneering— it pervades every facet of government.

CHAPTER ELEVEN

A jump toward a conclusion
OR,
Will 1984 be here before 1976?

Back at the beginning of this book, the claim that Richard Nixon had, through his election, "achieved a philosophical identity with some deep American values" was rejected. Perhaps that was too abrupt and, seen in a slightly different context, should be amended. In one narrow sense, Richard Nixon has connected with a dominant strand of American thought—the mini-max strategy. If there is one destructive feature of the U.S. political mind it is the belief that maximum accomplishments can be attained at minimum costs. During the sixties various political snake-oil salesmen made their appearance to be replaced by others in an unending stream. Each offered to cheering multitudes one unique version of a mini-max strategy and thus prepared the way for those who followed. Although coming in different sizes, shapes, and directions, each was kindred and offered the allure that—with a minimal expenditure of energy, limited

235

organization, limited funds, and limited time—great and wonderful things could be made to happen. Thus we find:

- In the early sixties a well-advertised campaign for a drug world. Tim Leary's siren call for the ultimate "in" mini-max strategies—"turn on, tune in, and drop out" —was followed by many variations on the theme, each considered kindly by publishers, rewarded by press coverage, and given access to platforms for presentation.

- In the middle of the decade, Charles Reich came forth with the widely acclaimed *The Greening of America*, read and discussed on every campus in the United States. Optimistically, Reich claimed that a revolution *was* in process, and persons served progress by merely waiting until the new, understanding "Consciousness III" sought him out. The evidence of this emerging new state could be seen everywhere, particularly in the new sartorial and tonsorial styles of Madison Avenue executives.

- Appealing particularly to the college crowd was Theodore Roszak and his *The Making of a Counter Culture*— here the analysis was that in the repugnance with what is an overemphasis on science, persons were creating viable new life styles in new communities which in time would be so attractive that only a few diehards would remain attached to the old ship—sort of a political version of Jack London's *The Sea Wolf*.

- Ivan Illich and all the rest who support in one form or another a *Deschooling Society* offer new breakthroughs merely through abolishing public schools.

- Alan Watts presented for your creative imagination the wondrous futures offered by *Zen Buddhism* and other forms of westernized eastern religions.

- And even the sometimes funny but mostly dreary obviously nonpolitical antics of the team of Abbie Hoffman and Jerry Rubin heralding a revolution without plan or planning was another easy way to accomplish nothing, as was the notion of so many that perhaps by sitting back and letting the most oppressed among us— the nonwhite minorities—lead us all to a political promised land we could vicariously identify with the Black Panthers or with those who so ruthlessly crushed them.

And Richard Nixon was the logical culmination of all this.

But the 1960s was not only a decade of homage to the unreal, it had an analog: the emergence of the cynic to heroic status. As the sixties struggled to a close and the seventies made a reluctant appearance, persons who concluded that problems were beyond solution gained in eminence. And thus we found—

- Edward Banfried suggesting repression and wage cutbacks for the *Unheavenly City*.
- Arthur Jensen and William Shockley postulating nonwhite genetic inferiority.
- Daniel Patrick Moynihan advocating "benign neglect" of the problems of the blacks.
- Christopher Jencks suggesting, on the basis of extremely limited data, that schools can do almost nothing about reducing inequality.
- Economists, political scientists, psychologists, sociologists, biologists, physicists, anthropologists, literally wallowing in what is wrong and offering virtually nothing to rectify the situation.
- Universities without a sense of the universe, professors with nothing to profess, and cynicism confused with scholarship.

The logical consequence of all this is Richard Nixon.

And that isn't all.

237

The sixties saw some significant changes in the political structure of the society:

- The labor unions got old and conservative.
- The Jewish community, torn by concern for Israel and curiously confronted by an emerging black awareness, also turned to conservatism.
- The political apparatus itself became technical and thus more expensive and remote. Thus it came to be that he who controlled the media controlled the nation. TV or not TV was no longer a question, it was imperative.

And the logical consequence of all this was Richard Nixon.

The sixties was not a decade of despair and inactivity. In the sixties there was political ferment and probably *more* youth actually involved in some effort to alter the direction of the country than *ever* before. But the efforts ran aground because—

- The major movements in the sixties which involved peace, poverty, racism, and environment were poorly planned and tended to ignore electoral politics.
- The movements not only didn't connect, but worked at cross-purposes.
- The movements were ad hoc, seemingly opposed to organization on principle and thus had little staying power.
- The movements were negatively oriented, opposing what is, instead of presenting well-researched proposals for remedies.
- The movements deflected from scholarship on the campus because, caught up in the emergency of the moment, they departed from central nervous system involvement and gave way to the sympathetic nervous system. If one slogan could capture the mood of the uni-

238

versity during the sixties, it was—"It is too late to think."

And Richard Nixon was the obvious consequence of all this.

That is where we are—Big Brother *is* watching us, so we ought to give him a good show.

The moves are relatively clear: either become discouraged by the failure of the sixties and retreat to the silence of the fifties (and that's what got Richard Nixon going on his triumphant ride) or get down to the serious business of developing maxi-max strategies, of paying the price for a society fit for human beings. This means that—

- On campus, students become students by planning and testing out models for the future.
- Everyone gets with *some* political organization, pays dues, and gets involved in policy determination and candidate selection.
- No one is allowed a free ride, everyone is challenged to put his money where his mouth is.
- The issues of the sixties—war-peace, environmental protection, equality, and relief from poverty—*are* recognized as the big problems and political programs are tied to them.
- Everyone is held accountable and must defend his views with logic and evidence before *all* critics. No longer should persons comfortably secluded miles away from social problems be credited with expert status just because others equally removed applaud them.

The situation facing us is no more desperate than the emergencies of the past. The democracy we claim has always been imperfect; people have been mercilessly oppressed and denied justice. In dealing with that oppression, there were

239

exciting progress and heart-rending defeats. What we face today is a different set of circumstances. It is more difficult only because it is larger, more technical, more mysterious. A society lives as its people grow to meet new challenges. The challenges will be met—

- Through new approaches to public education, with each of us striving both to hear and to be heard.
- Through involvement in electoral politics. *Now* is the time to be involved in the next elections in your community.
- Through insistence that your servants, your elected officials, make their presence known to you.

The future will go to those who *work* hard enough, in spite of discouragement, to get it and who, while working, take a little time out to dream about a world that could be and what would be the first steps to get there.

Work is the key to a better world and work is created by human beings, so perhaps first steps would be government using its influence to create meaningful jobs for the troubled and the troublesome.

The issues are there, it is time for the debate to begin,
        and 1976
            is
            almost
                here!